MASARYK
ON THOUGHT AND LIFE

Conversations with
Karel Čapek

MASARYK
ON THOUGHT AND LIFE

Conversations with
Karel Čapek

Translated from the Czech by
M. & R. WEATHERALL

LONDON
GEORGE ALLEN & UNWIN LTD
MUSEUM STREET

FIRST PUBLISHED IN 1938
SECOND IMPRESSION 1944

CONTENTS

I

EPISTEMOLOGY—THE THEORY OF KNOWLEDGE

1 . *On Knowledge*

YOU enquire of my philosophy, my epistemology, and metaphysics — yes, in their literal sense I have not worked them out systematically, only now and again have I written this or that; I have formulated them for foro interno, that, of course, is understood. Every man has his own philosophy, or if you like, his own metaphysics. Let me explain to you first: I have never pretended to be a philosopher, not to say a metaphysician.

And so speaks a professor of philosophy!

True! I used to teach the history of philosophy, the philosophy of history, I taught sociology; yes, in them I did bring in my philosophy, my metaphysics, but I did not lecture, or write of it as a whole. Psychology, ethics, the philosophy of law, philosophy of history, sociology, and so on, are often included in philosophy, but that is an erroneous system for classifying the sciences. These are all specialized, independent sciences, or parts of independent sciences. Of course, every specialized science has its own philosophical foundations, its close relation to philosophy. Of real philosophical sciences there are only two: logic, including epistemology, and metaphysics. Philosophy—with this word one conceives on the one hand some sort of wisdom, some deeper understanding and knowledge, and on the other a general conception of the world and of life. For me philosophy, I mean scientific philosophy, is an attempt to achieve a general conception of the world, inclusive of the mind; it should be the sum total of all knowledge, the synthesis of all sciences—but can anyone today comprehend all the sciences, developed into such specializations? Well, it is impossible even if one were ever so learned. That is the grave problem: what is, what can philosophy be, or metaphysics, beside the specialized sciences.

And there is the problem whether philosophy and metaphysics are a science.

Not that! Philosophy, and, therefore, metaphysics too, cannot be anything else but scientific, they must never, on any account, be in conflict with scientific knowledge. If I call it a problem, I mean by that a task; that task is clear, but to solve it is difficult; in it the last word will never be said, just as the last word will never be said in human knowledge.

EPISTEMOLOGY

But to give you an answer: my philosophy, my epistemology, and metaphysics are implicit in my literary works; they are also bound up with my actions and the way in which I have acted——

or they are bound up with their practical applications. In that, Mr. President, you are something of a pragmatist.

Pragmatist—not that! But of the pragmatists, there are also several; in so far as they include Pierce, or William James, these two derive from Kant, and by this already they are alien to me. Also I have never attached such importance to utilitarianism, and even with regard to religion, I stand on other ground. James wrote that pragmatism is only a new name for old ways of thinking—I don't like new names for old things.

It is true that there are several kinds of pragmatism; but I should also say that there is a Czech form of pragmatism. For instance, the typical Czech thinkers: Komenský, Palacký, Havlíček—Havlíček too is a philosopher. I know that you can't put them into one bunch; but what strikes the eye is that all the time these three turn their thoughts to the practical things of life, to the things of life of the nation. All three are politicians. In fact typical Czech philosophy is political—perhaps because a small nation cannot allow itself the luxury of thinking for thinking's sake.

Well then, I should call this Czech pragmatism, or the practical tradition of Czech philosophy; and within this tradition I should also include you.

Well that's true, you can point to these three; they lectured but they also gave a practical lead; and their politics—they were an urge to regenerate the nation through education and humanity, to liberate the race politically and spiritually. And it is significant that all three had a world outlook. Komenský, a typical Czech, with a spirit already fairly modern: he was a religiously minded man, and he lived his faith also as a teacher and as a politician. The apostle of humanity, the preacher of harmony in everything, and everywhere; he worked for the nation through his work for the whole world, and he moved all about in that world. He is acknowledged as a teacher of the nations—the first genuine and conscious Pan-European.

Palacký—he delved into the history of our race, and he gave us a well-grounded philosophy of our history: from that he deduced the principles of our politics, and in politics he took an active part. In him is nicely exemplified the old historia vitae magistra.

And Havlíček—a modern spirit, energetic, but ever cautious, critical, conscious of his responsibility to the nation; in short, a model for a democratic journalist. He followed Palacký, for a time he was also a deputy; in this way he was a living example of how journalism and politics are associated. You are right, he was a philosopher too—after all it is not only professors who are philosophers, every thinking man has some philosophy of his own, some metaphysics, an attempt to grasp the sense of life and of the world. And with Havlíček every word, every article is an expression of the complete world view.

Our tradition in philosophy you say. I don't know, one does not admit it clearly enough; but I can say that in those three I have found my own, and also our national programme; time and again I have tested my views on them. You emphasize the practical side of my philosophy. That may be! I always liked to work, and I tried to be practical, my thoughts were turned to practice, and put into practice; but there is no practice without theory. Theory need not be formulated by itself, it is enough if it underlies and directs practice.

Theory then for the sake of practice.

Yes, but also practice for the sake of theory. Theory is of value, even if it cannot immediately be applied in practice. To understand is just as important as to act. Through action we obtain knowledge, just as through obtaining knowledge we prepare for the right action. If there is a conflict sometimes between theory and practice then there is a mistake somewhere: either the theory is bad, or the practice, often both. With my practical nature, I am all the time for theory, for pure scientific and philosophical knowledge. I am not in favour of barren speculation, of playing with words, I am not in favour of bad practice, and of needless labour—just as theory may bear no flower, so practice may bear no fruit. Work and utility are not the meaning of life— the devil is very industrious, he is up to his tricks night and day, and yet he is stupid. Our Czech and Slovak devil. At any rate, I am for objectivity, for knowledge of concrete things. Not pragmatism but concretism would be my motto.

This brings us nearly to the point where we were before. In the place of the duality of theory and practice you put the duality of concrete and abstract knowledge.

No — the discrepancy between abstract and concrete knowledge is only a matter of logic. Knowledge of things, of details, knowledge of the concrete is based on knowledge of the abstract. For example: you have an abstract psychology which deals with the mind and consciousness, with ideas, judgements, feelings, will, imagination, memory. Yes, but all these categories do not exist by themselves, do they, they are merely abstractions; in a living man all these different kinds of elements, and activities are combined together in one unity. Every man is a whole world, a microcosm, and no two men are alike; think of the different temperaments, characters, and talents, sexual differences, differences of age, professional, national, and racial differences! Already we have got a concrete psychology too, for instance, the psychology of childhood, of genius, of art, and religion, the psychology of personality, and so forth. But before that there had to be abstract knowledge so that we could classify, and work out systematically that concrete reality of psychological detail. On grounds of evolution and logic, knowledge of the abstract precedes knowledge of the concrete.

At least in so far as scientific knowledge is concerned.

Yes; but every real, systematic act of obtaining knowledge is scientific, or at least it attempts to be scientific. There is no antagonism between abstract and concrete knowledge, the relation is purely a matter of logic and method; both types of knowledge arise from the study of the same objects, that is of concrete things.

Take this example: in Nature life does not exist, only living individualities; men exist, animals, plants. In accordance with these classes we have anthropology, zoology, and botany; but besides these sciences, and logically preceding them comes biology, the abstract science of life itself. You are something of a gardener, and you know how much you would miss of the beauty, and comprehension of Nature if you did not know at least something of the abstract biology of plants, if you did not know something of their structure, of their propagation, their composition, chemistry, and so on. If we did not follow the way of abstract knowledge, we should stand as if partly blind before the world of concrete detail.

The true object of knowledge is the world of details, individuals, of individualities living and non-living; but that knowledge we reach by the roundabout way of abstract sciences. To know means to obtain the most exact and complete knowledge of concrete reality; for this very thing it is first necessary to abstract, construct theoretically, and reduce to a scientific system the constituent elements, and general laws of things, and of all kinds of processes—but we must not forget that the real aim and object of knowledge is that world of individual beings and things which, and only which, is given to us.

Which is given to us—for what? For our knowledge, or for our actions?

For both, for action and for knowing—you

cannot act without knowledge. Even the obtaining of knowledge is an activity, often an activity of immense energy, or, as we say, creative. One speaks of a technical age, one says that the modern type of man is a technician, and not a thinker; but where would technical work be without the tremendous theoretical work that preceded it?

To search for knowledge, that, sir, is an extremely active life. When you say science you also mean by it effort, patience, persistence, devotion, honesty—nothing but the requirements of an active life—and of a moral life.

In this are you subordinating science to ethics?

I should say: not science but the scientist. To ethics every man is subordinated, and completely, everything that he lives, and does, and then what he comprehends. To comprehend is a moral duty, just the same as the love and service of one's neighbour, just the same as any of the moral prescriptions. We do not honour the talents of the scientists and philosophers, but their great struggle for the truth—that is the moral act. Therefore, we also feel the misuse of science is a sin, it is a sin against the Holy Ghost. The morality and usefulness of science lies in the fact that it goes absolutely, purely, and strictly for knowledge, for truth; but every truth is, or will at some time be, good for life.

Yes, but perhaps it depends on the way in which one makes use of this truth.

By that you wish to say that sometimes one misuses, or makes wrong use of science and knowledge. Yes. In spite of that I should say: truth before all things, truth always and everywhere. Truth is never in conflict with morality; no lie, or untruth is permanently good, not even the so-called fraus pia. We have life, we have views, and convictions, we have social relations oppressed with a mess of lies, and more than that, needless ones. A lie is unmanly; it is the weapon of weaklings, often enough of brutal—not of strong men. Truth, honest truth, real knowledge, can never do harm.

And what about the science that serves war?

Science does not make war, but men, human imperfections, men not giving science sufficiently its due; if the world were guided more by knowledge and truth there would be less of those wars, nay, there need even be none at all. For defence it is right and proper to make use of science; but to cultivate science for violence, for aggressive warfare, is a crime. In the end we must discriminate between right and violence, truth and falsity, reality and fiction, in those cases also where previously men resorted to arms. I think that the last great war proved clearly enough the needlessness, harmfulness, and stupidity of warfare.

Of course, our present knowledge of the world and of men is still far from complete, but just because of that let us strive honestly and persistently for knowledge, for truth! And truth is victorious.

2. *What is Truth?*

But then it seems to me that from epistemology we have passed over to ethics.

Not quite, we are on the way. You began with pragmatism, and the pragmatist builds his theory of knowledge on the needs of practical life. In this way we come to the relation between theory and practice. I deny this dualism: a man is not divided into one half that knows, and another half that acts: through action he obtains knowledge, obtaining knowledge itself is work and action——and what a powerful activity, sir! Epistemology asks what knowledge is, what truth is. Ethics must ask whether we serve truth as honestly and completely as we ought to do.

Well, all right: what is truth?

Ah, Pilate's question. Will you please tell me what those birds are in the park?

Magpies, Mr. President.

Your eyes are better. Aren't they pigeons?
No, magpies.

Do you know that for certain?
I do. I have been looking at them already quite a time, and carefully. Pigeons fly differently.

So you see, you yourself quoted the marks of truth: that you know for certain because you have been looking carefully, and I have verified my knowledge with yours. Since at all costs you require a definition of truth, I should say, truth is what we know for certain, and critically, reality brought to consciousness. That is the whole thing: what we know we know without doubt; and with certainty, at least with all the certainty attainable at the time. As Aristotle said: man desires knowledge of Nature—yes; but it is just that certain and sure knowledge that he desires. The urge for certainty, the urge for conviction, and for truth: that is the foundation, and the sense of all epistemology, nothing else.

You said that in my writings you did not find any elaborate criticism and theory of knowledge, no epistemology of my own. I might say that it is there; but that you need not look for it, I will point it out to you, of course, only the key-words. I hardly feel that I shall ever again find myself teaching ex cathedra on the problems and system of epistemology. Bear in mind that I grew away from Plato, fought my way through Hume's scepticism, Kant's subjectivism, learned from Comte, Mill, Brentano, and many more besides —how many questions in epistemology there are that I had to settle for myself!

Well, then, quite briefly: to every individual item of knowledge, to knowledge in general, to truth in general we come through thinking. Man is a thinking being besides having will and consciousness.

Thinking: that is, perceiving and imagining things—material and immaterial—by means of the senses, and of imagination, and secondly it is the contemplation of the things imagined. You see some black and white things that move: in your opinion already they are magpies. Truth lies in judgement, not in imagination. We argue about things we have imagined, we have our opinions, our convictions about them. This is the positive thing that from a mere conception creates a piece of knowledge.

Then a piece of knowledge is a judgement combined with conviction.

Or this: a piece of knowledge is a conscious judgement, a judgement that consciously strives for truth, certainty, and security. In forming a judgement we testify that we believe in something, and in so doing, that we are convinced of something. Conviction is well founded belief; we say that we are sure of this or that, absolutely sure, that we have certain knowledge of it. In a word: certainty.

To strive for certainty: that means to observe carefully that on which we pass judgement, to be attentive, to be critical. Knowledge is critical consciousness. To think, to obtain knowledge, to know, that means to bring well into consciousness, what we know, and what we don't know, what we have comprehended, what we are ignorant of, what we cannot know. A critical attitude does not mean hesitation, indecision, dubiety, or scepticism. To be critical, that is, to investigate, to test, to control, to verify the data of knowledge. This at least is one criterion of truth: truth is a judgement which has passed through the testing fire of criticism.

And not merely of our criticism. All scientific knowledge is continually being subjected to the supervision, and criticism of innumerable people; it can be, and always is being verified, corrected, or confirmed. Not only is there an increase in the facts of knowledge but also in critical methods; just think what a quantity of experimentation and of measurement we have today! Criticism of others, and continual criticism, that great collaboration in the search for truth is also one of the guarantees of our knowledge. We cannot believe that we already possess enough knowledge, and nothing but the truth; but we can be sure —and this also is an epistemological certainty, that through the progress of the ages we shall approach ever nearer and nearer to truth.

3. On Myth

I say again: a critical attitude is not scepticism. Doubt is not the origin of thought as it is sometimes held to be.

Not for the very reason that scepticism evolved late.

Well yes. By nature man is trusting, I should say credulous. He believes his senses, imagination, and memory, he has faith in his reason, feelings, efforts, and will, he believes not only in himself but also in others; he believes blindly, childishly, naïvely. You know what uncritical faith men can have even today; then what about primitive man! A savage does not distinguish between reality, and the products of phantasy, dreams, visions, fictions, surmises, analogies; he acts impulsively, and impulsively, unrestrainedly he also thinks. His explanation of the world and of life is a mixture of experience, and of fragments

23

of knowledge associated with uncritical cogitation, and with traditions that have been handed down. It is, I should say, a spiritual state of absolutism; the primitive man politically is blindly subject to his leader, spiritually to the priests. This epistemological state I should call mythical—in the mythology of the primitive races it shows quite clearly.

In myths the process is by analogy. A primitive man explains the whole world in terms of himself, in terms of his consciousness, and the functions of his body, in terms of his nearest surroundings, his tribe, altogether in terms of his experience. A man disposed to believe in myth is a naïve egocentric, and egoist, he is not a puzzle to himself, and the world is no puzzle to him.

In fact, an egoist who does not observe himself.

A primitive man is completely immersed in his surroundings, he is an absolute objectivist; man looks with more attention into himself much later on. A man from the country even today is more objective than one from the town, a workman more than an intellectual; a child is so immersed in a thing that for a long time it is not conscious of itself. Only at a more advanced age, so to speak, does man look into himself, not merely round him. At first he projects his ego

24

into his surroundings, this occurs spontaneously, without criticism, and without purpose, quite naïvely. In the events around him, and in the motion of things, primitive man looks for forces similar to those that influence him; from the analogy of his ego he sees living and active beings, spirits, idols, and gods in things which change, or he puts them behind and above these things as the agents and masters of things. Arranging these mythical conceptions into mythological systems, that already is a further development of thought; for that you must realize that primitive man took thousands of years, they constitute a larger process of development than science——no wonder that so much mythology also persists in our thoughts and conceptions. Think of it, the Greeks and the Romans, if I remember rightly, had more than three thousand superhuman, transcendental deities, and semi-deities of all kinds. Primitive man is interested in the world as a whole; he cannot help asking where the world has come from, and what will happen to it, he meditates about himself, and about his fate, where he has come from, how he was born, how life is sustained, what is the meaning of death; he must have some conception of the society in which and with which he lives——in short, man from the earliest times has had some sort of Weltanshaung, some view of life, he has had some sort of philosophy. A primitive, mythical one———

and as old as the stone tools.

But it has not been lost, my friend, it is buried in us like those stone knives, arrows, and axes in the ground. When we know more about present man, we shall find a trace of his original myths. In us there is still a very great deal of that naïve egocentricity, of that faith in idols, and bogies; if you want evidences, you will find them easily —in politics, perhaps.

4. *Knowledge and Myth*

Well then: along with that mythological disposition, and contrary to it, there develops in man knowledge—we can already call it critical, scientific. The life of primitive man as we know today was hard, it was no paradise, it was no Saturnian golden age; man had to learn to observe, to perceive, to judge; in short, to think; he had to produce and improve his tools so as to preserve the life of himself and of his kindred. Even the simplest tool is already a piece of mechanics and physics; hunting, herd-keeping, and agriculture are the beginnings of zoology, botany, astronomy, and of other things besides. From the very beginnings man had to struggle to live—and work; that means to learn, to make experiments, to invent, and to rise above himself, and above his surroundings. Exact thought originated with the most ordinary and practical things; only later were the myths of the more unusual, uncommon, and imaginary ones overcome. We may say that the conflict between critical thought and naïve credulity, between knowledge and faith, between science and myth is as old as man, as old as mankind.

Very likely in prehistoric times there was already a conflict between progress and conservatism.

Certainly there was. As a conception of life, and of the world, as an attempt to explain the world and life, in an evolutionary sense—in the individual and in society—myth is more ancient, more original than criticism and science, credulity is more deeply rooted in men than the critical attitude; therefore, from the historical standpoint of this conflict, myth seems to be positive, critical science negative, because it corrects and, in fact, denies and destroys all primitive mythical views. You will find an understanding of the conflict between science and myth that is modern enough in Vico, who drew up three stages of development: poetic, heroic, and human; this triple phase was accepted by Turgot, and Saint-Simon. After them you have Comte maintaining that human culture as a whole passes through three phases: theological — with the stages in development of fetishism, polytheism, and monotheism—metaphysical, which in place of the deities puts abstract notions, and at last positivist, scientific which instead of searching for first causes, ascertains the facts, their order, and laws.

Ad vocem Comte: he began with a criticism of myth, and he ended with a complete positivist mythology created out of his own phantasy. In him one sees how deeply myth is rooted in man.

As a writer I should say, thank God. We authors in fact cannot exist without mythology.

Nor can we philosophers, sir. A poet differs from a scientist, and from a philosopher, although philosophy was rather aptly called a conceptual novel: a poet, an artist, thinks in pictures, and a philosopher in concepts. But even a scientist cannot manage without phantasy, or, to use Goethe's terminology: without exact phantasy. The spiritual development of an individual, and of society, lies in the very fact that step by step the credulous myth is being forsaken, and critical knowledge is being accepted. Mythology gives place to science, but in science the traces of myth persist, and even new myths are being created—

what do we want, a man loves myths, mythology and science in him are not kept sharply distinct, they interact. In philosophy you have more myth because science restricts itself to its sphere, while philosophy embraces all spheres, the whole of life and of the world. A primitive man, in his theory, in his explanation of life and of the world, is too impetuous; the man with a critical and scientific mind becomes more modest, he knows how little he knows. And in common life—the same medley. If you examine contemporary society, you will find in it, existing closely side by side, the most diverse ranges and types of myth and science, you will find absolute primitivism.

As someone I can no longer remember has said: primitive and medieval man are both alive in us——

Yes, and also the men of antiquity, Socrates, Plato, Aristotle are alive, and not these alone: in modern man there is living not only the past, but also the future. Evolution—in Nature and in man—is not all change, it is also the preservation of the old, and the creation of the new, the future.

Do not forget: myths have been orginating for thousands and thousands of years—therefore, they are collective, traditional, and it was easy for them to obtain popular assent. On the contrary, criticism, science, as a new process is individual, it is born of personal talent, and of personal experience—at a higher stage of culture, therefore, popular assent arises far less easily. Science is not collective, but co-operative; and you know, co-operation is always, in thought as well as in practice, more difficult than spontaneous, general assent. The conflict between critical knowledge and mythical faith appears in all history as a conflict of individuals and minorities with the majority.

You need only look into the history of philosophy, beginning with the Greeks: how soon after Homer and Hesiod, after the creators and glorifiers of myths, philosophy originates which no longer explains the world in terms of gods, and attempts to deduce it from one empirical principle—from water, from air, from some kind of primordial substance: you have Thales, Anaximenes, Anaximandros, and from a number: the Pythagoreans—again new myths. Nota bene, right in those earliest beginnings you see that abstractness of which we were speaking. Later on the plurality of principles is accepted as the explanation of the world: Empedocles, Anaxagoras and Democritus already compose the universe out of elements, atoms, and at the same time systematic reason is coming into operation, Nus—in Anaxagoras; this is the beginning of the philosophical teaching of finality of the universal order, the beginning of theism, and monotheism. And it is important that these early philosophers, and all the others after them, whether expressly, or somewhat by implication, took up a stand against mythology, against the more or less rigid theology of popular religion. Hence the aversion of the priests, too frequently the official mythologians, to philosophy and science—in Anaxagoras, in Socrates we have the first victims of this conflict between knowledge and blind faith. And it is conceivable that with the so-called Sophists scepticism, individualism, and subjectivism were also present to a certain extent. At first philosophers occupied themselves with the external world, not until later with the inner world—Socrates, as has been said, brought philosophy down to earth from heaven; originally man was a radical objectivist, only later does he also turn his attention to the subject, to his own heart.

Along with philosophy the specialized sciences developed, medicine, and above all mathematics —it is, sir, no accident that from the Greeks only one single text-book has come down to us, and that one is on mathematics and geometry by Euclid. Here again you see the primacy of abstract knowledge. And the specialized sciences were still more antagonistic to myth than philosophy.

31

True: but what you are telling me is more of a history of knowledge than a theory of knowledge.

I don't think so. Tracing the history of knowledge also means to understand the ways of knowledge. Yes, a history of knowledge, but an eternal history which is going on all the time, and for ever. This conflict between credulity and criticism, between myth and knowledge is a product of our human nature; it is by this conquest of myth that knowledge itself is characterized, and defined.

Knowledge! I ask you, it is a word just as abstract as nature, or life. What today we call knowledge, science, consists of innumerable pieces of information of individual men—and mainly perhaps of those of whom not even the name has survived. Our knowledge, our culture is based on the sum of countless personal achievements, and the discoveries of nameless minds, nameless geniuses; we only continue their work: I often meditate on those unknown thinkers of primeval times, and of all ages—how much they must have thought out and done, so that even we too now may philosophize so comfortably.

The development of the human knowledge took place, still does, and will continue to do so by that antithesis of scientific exactness and myth; science is the concensus of thinking men, thinking exactly, and critically; every item of knowledge travels from head to head, from man to man, from one age to another, to be tested, corrected, and increased. Knowledge is nothing complete, it is a living, unfinished work, it is a continual process of obtaining knowledge. We know more, and more exactly than was known a hundred, than a thousand years ago; who can say what men will discover, and comprehend in a hundred, in a thousand, in a hundred thousand years hence. We must not forget that that development of exactitude is only in its beginnings. Scientists and philosophers often enumerate problems which they say human understanding will never solve, which are beyond the frontiers, and beyond the range of our knowledge. But where is the final barrier of knowledge, where will it be one day? That there will be one is certain: but it is equally certain that as long as man thinks he will move it further and further away. The evolution of thought itself, and the development of reflection gives us one epistemological guarantee: faith in more perfect knowledge in the future.

5. Problems of Knowledge

That's true; but no faith in better knowledge in the future will do away with the need for us also *to have some epistemological guarantees for the present.*

Of course. We want to know, we have to know what knowledge is valid, correct, and safe. Actually we have a double guarantee that the knowledge we obtain is correct. The first I should call an ethical guarantee: the correctness of our knowledge is guaranteed by our truthfulness, seriousness, intellectual honesty; we desire nothing but the truth, we work for truth all the time, and at all times we are willing to recognize our mistakes, verify our facts, or accept correct information. The other guarantee is rational: it is that critical attitude of which we already have spoken; we shall only hold that to be true that has stood the test of scrutiny, of objective and careful criticism, as we say, of objective criticism. But I know that these practical guarantees are not sufficient to clear away epistemological scruples.

When you dip the end of a stick into water, it seems to you that the stick is broken; it is an optical delusion which we subsequently correct by further experience. We know that experience may make mistakes, our senses and reason may make mistakes too; therefore, a man who is critical and thoughtful falls into a strange uneasiness, he knows that he may make a mistake. He enquires, and must enquire whether things are

34

really the same as we see, and experience them through our senses, as we imagine them and as we reason about them. He asks what they are, what is the reality of those things, and what is, of what kind is, our process of obtaining knowledge. Is our knowledge objective, that is, does it more or less correspond with the things as they really are? Or is it subjective, that is, more or less conditioned by our senses, our experiences, powers of reason? What in our conceptions, judgements, and items of knowledge is objective, what subjective? These are the questions from which springs the whole of epistemology—and also ultimately metaphysical speculation.

In a naïve epistemological state man imagines that through his senses he perceives things as they really are, that things are simply mirrored in us. Later on, with better observation, he discovers that our senses are bound to make mistakes, that our senses and mind do not depict things quite exactly; and by further and better observation of himself, he becomes aware that in perceiving the subject is not merely passive, merely receptive, but that he works actively on the images that he receives from outside. For instance: beyond us, "outside" are not general concepts, but individual, and concrete things; and yet without general concepts we cannot think, or obtain

35

knowledge. In the evolution of philosophy this led to the idea that the ego, spirit, consciousness, subject is not a mirror but something active, something that more or less creates of itself our items of knowledge. Our knowledge at any rate is partly subjective, it is the work of our minds. Or to use the slang of the philosophers, to the old, original objectivism, epistemological subjectivism became added. Hence arise those conflicts between different epistemological theories: either they are more or less objective, realistic—our knowledge being caused and conditioned by things external to us, by objects, by objective reality; or subjective, idealistic, as one says—all knowledge being the product of our minds.

You know that the decisive turn to his subjectivism and idealism was given by Kant, and by the philosophers after Kant. What Copernicus achieved in astronomy Kant did in epistemology: knowledge does not conform to the objects, but the objects conform to our knowledge; what we take to be the external world, reality, is the product of our subjectivity. It is only a step in time from subjectivism to solipsism: Only myself, solus ipse, I alone am the creator of the world, the world is my idea. Kant and the German idealists overtrumped the superman and created the supercreator. Funny, how the human mind can be so conceited. Extreme subjectivism, I should say, is betrayal by the philosophers, betrayal by educated men as a whole.

From this I see that you profess epistemological realism, objectivism.

Yes. How otherwise? A man who desires to act, to act in a practical way, and with responsibility, cannot be a subjectivist. I acknowledge the objective world. Things external to us that we try to comprehend are approximately such as they appear to our experience.

This, of course, is a metaphysical assertion.

That is understood; but any other assertion is also metaphysical. I say "approximately"—we approach things by our process of knowledge; we know them better and more accurately than we did a thousand years ago, we shall approach them always nearer.

The other thing that is the object of epistemological investigation is the knowing subject. What in reality is that subject, in which way does it obtain knowledge? Surely through the senses and by experience; but also through comparison and memory, also through reason—in reality man as a whole obtains knowledge, not merely his individual faculties. And besides—which of these faculties gives us the most reliable and least fallible knowledge? In accordance with this you again have various philosophical schools and conflicts: only that knowledge is held to be certain and reliable which can be controlled by the senses —sensualism; or based on experience as a whole —empiricism. Others point to the deceptiveness of the senses, and seek certainty only in reason —rationalism: Others accept both experience and reason—intellectualism. Recent psychology has shown how in all mental acts feeling and will exert their influence; in our knowledge also we are directed by them—one speaks of knowledge through feeling—emotionalism, and through the will—voluntarism. You see what a choice there is.

And your own standpoint?

My own standpoint—above all, as I have said: not to forget that in every act of knowledge, the whole man is concerned. Every radical epistemological theory which accepts only one aspect to the detriment of the others is erroneous. We must proceed from knowledge as it is really formed. And remember that all our knowledge has been provided by the mental efforts of innumerable generations. We all participate in this work; do we not even from our mothers learn words, language; through words we obtain concepts, the condensed experiences of millions of minds.

EPISTEMOLOGY

Well then: psychology and the psychological genesis of knowledge in place of epistemology?

Not that! The psychology of knowledge can tell us how we obtain knowledge, but whether that knowledge is right and certain truth, that it can't say. The analysis and description of the process of knowledge, however good, will not tell us what knowledge is correct. Epistemology is not psychology, but part of logic which enquires what we know to be right and certain.

Well: as a foundation for the whole of knowledge, I accept the whole man. I accept reason and the senses, I recognize also feelings and will, altogether the whole of experience; also through feeling, sympathy, and effort a reasonable man finds the kernel of truth, sometimes more than a kernel. But the duality of reason and the senses, not that. Reason and experience are complimentary to each other. True: experience of the senses is unreliable, but it is supervised and checked by reason. Reason might err, but it is again checked by experience.

So rationalism after all.

Rationalism too, in both senses, nothing against reason, nothing above reason. For certain and true I hold those data of knowledge which are in harmony with experience and reason. But both of these, experience and reason, are in no way complete; we have not enough of them yet that would allow us to set their limits. Our knowledge is only at the beginning——

and, therefore, even our theory of knowledge cannot last for ever.

Look at the development of knowledge: every step forward in knowledge has its own epistemology; our theory of knowledge can only correspond with that stage of development that has been reached by our knowledge of the world. And that it is not the final stage, that we know for certain. But faith in the possibility and value of knowledge, an unshakable and active faith has been held by strong spirits of all ages.

6. *Irrationalism*

Well then, that epistemological development of mankind: the oldest theory, after all, is that for our existence the certain and most important knowledge, in fact, all knowledge taken as a whole, was revealed to man; the certainty and irrefutability of knowledge is guaranteed by the highest authority, by the Godhead itself.

Then the Negro sorcerer also has his own epistemology when he asserts that through his mouth a spirit speaks.

40

EPISTEMOLOGY

Well, he has not got much of that epistemology —but what he does possess is a system of knowledge of his own; he is the typical irrationalist. Direct revelation is usually conferred on some chosen individual——a priest, a prophet, and from him other men accept it passively, blindly, obediently. Faith in supernatural revelation is still and perpetually alive. It would, you know, be strange if God had only revealed himself to man in biblical times. There are people to be found also today who look upon themselves as the agent for some superrational and higher revelation. And besides that, some peculiar mental states are taken for some kind of quasi-revelation; unusually gifted, prominent personalities tend even today to be accepted as if they were the instruments, or voice of some higher intelligence——not in religion only, but also in art, in politics, and elsewhere. To this you can also add faith in inspiration; mysticism comes in here, an appearance of direct communion with the Godhead; modern occultism also comes in here, faith in premonition, and other mysterious intimations. In the end you also find certain varieties of faith in revelation in the prominent modern philosophers: what else are James's exceptional experiences, what else Bergson's intuition, what is the irrationalism preached in our days? And what otherwise is the most recent nationalism claiming the "healthy instinct" of a nation as the supreme law?

That is it: people are not content with their own reason and judgement, they must find some authority in an epistemological sense often rather dubious; they long to have faith and certainty no matter what kind it is. Thence comes blind faith, superstition, ecclesiasticism; thence — in politics—mythical and mystical faith in collective slogans. The masses, the times, desire this and that, they demand so and so, and there it is. A comfortable theory also for dictators and demagogues. Of course, one must distinguish here between two things. Collective concepts like nation, state, church, class, spirit of the time, to the majority of people are too complex, or rather beyond their imagination; they must reduce them to some formula which they then take to be the valid expression of the community: in actual fact they merely anthropomorphize primitively, as their ancestors did, heaven, nature, and so on. And that collective mysticism is often nothing more than mass egoism—say, the egoism of a group, party, or class. People who speak in the name of the nation, or of the times, attribute to themselves the only proper feeling and understanding for the nation, fatherland, the times; others, chiefly the more critical ones, according to them do not possess the proper feeling and understanding, they are reactionaries, traitors, and so on. You know that epistemology of that type in politics is still rampant, and not only in our own case.

It would not be fair not to mention that that political primitivism to a certain extent is provided with weapons by those philosophers and psychologists who put feeling and will—instinct as well—against and above reason—the emotionalists, and voluntarists. And yet in every textbook of elementary psychology pupils can read that there is no feeling and will without ideas and judgements, that there is no pure feeling and will then, and that feelings differ according to their quality. A criminal also has feelings, he is driven and compelled by feelings and by will. Feelings and will are no argument if reason is lacking. How and by what means shall we decide which of the conflicting things, which of the contradictory wills is better and more correct? Again by reason and criticism.

And not only out of feelings and will is such a superrational authority being created, but also out of instincts, if an epitheton ornans is added: the healthy, natural, irresistible, then the most powerful epistemology and ethics are in a fix. Notice what stupidity some writers commit with sexual instinct, some demagogues with the national

43

instinct, with the elemental aversion to something, and that sort of thing: a strange psychology, and still stranger epistemology.

True: man is not only a rational being endowed with reason alone. As Pascal said, the heart has its reasons, reasons which reason does not understand.

I need not tell you that I do not abandon reason in any sphere; but reason is not the whole of spiritual life—besides it and with it, we have feelings and will. Feelings, volition, instincts force themselves upon our attention by their, as one says, elemental and spontaneous nature, whereas reason strikes one as sober, indifferent, and so on. Reason is cold, feelings are warm, boiling, burning, as one says pictorially, they give life its colour, they give pleasure, and happiness; sadness, of course, and misery too. pleasure, but unhappiness as well. Feelings are more apparent than the activities of reason, they are more vivid, and more insistent. Therefore, we say: "My feelings told me. I felt this and that." Psychologically it is different; with knowledge feeling was associated—a feeling of satisfaction, repulsion, amazement, or something else—this has become fixed in consciousness, and in memory more than the reasoning process. So-called knowledge through feeling tends to be simple knowledge through reason but accompanied with strong feeling. Is it not the perceiving and reasoning activities which give feelings, will, and suchlike things, their imaginative content? The man wills SOMETHING, through feeling he aims at SOME-THING. That something is not created either by feeling or by will, it is given by observation, imagination, experience, reason; that something may be right or wrong, possible or impossible—and to decide this is a matter of reason, and of reason alone.

And as for revelation—a pure heart and a clear mind put us in touch with reality. I do not recognize any supernatural revelation.

7 *Rationalism*

It was Plato who combined epistemological mysticism with rationalism, that is with radical rationalism, and after him came others. According to Plato the senses do not apprehend, only reason does that; not experience but general concepts constitute real knowledge. But whereabouts in us, creatures of the senses, Plato enquires, have the general concepts arisen? Plato was a weak psychologist, and, therefore, he had only this one answer: Abstract concepts, abstract knowledge, are nothing but the remembrance, anamnesis of ideas which the soul in its pre-corporal life perceived in the realm of eternal ideas, that is, in metaphysical reality. Material, concrete things only remind us of those eternal ideas which our soul beheld before we were born as human beings. In Plato we have a nice example of what we have already been speaking about: first the priority of abstract thought; then the beginnings of criticism—he takes exception to the unreliability of the senses; mythology—he anthropomorphizes concepts into some sort of higher entities, ideas; at last also turning back to the subject—he enquires where in us the concepts arise. Plato was the true father of philosophy; that is the reason why he had such an influence on philosophy—and still has. After him the Neo-Platonist Plotinus gathered together and embodied these ideas in the eternal Nus, the cosmic reason, from which our spirit "emanates," is enlightened by it, and filled with knowledge. Saint Augustine followed Plotinus, but in Nus he understood God; Plato's ideas become divine thoughts, our understanding is the divine enlightenment. An interesting connection between rationalism and the epistemology of revelation.

Aristotle, the industrious disciple of Plato, was scientifically more critical, he also sought for a more empirical psychology. He brought Plato's ideas from the supernatural realm of ideas down to earth, and put them into concrete things; ideas are the substance or kernel of things. Knowledge springs from the empirical, from concrete perception, but reason stimulated by the senses penetrates to the substance of entity. You can see how Aristotle struggled with Plato's myth; his semi-mythical philosophy and epistemology were taken over by the Medieval Church; Thomas Aquinas is an Aristotelian, Augustine is a Platonist.

The new philosophy—Descartes, Herbert of Cherbury, Leibniz, and others—found a secure foundation for our knowledge in innate ideas. Our fundamental conceptions of God, morality, and so on, do not come from our sense-experience, or from the activities of reason, but they are inborn in us, and this endows them with a higher and indubitable validity. But: why should innate ideas have such an absolute validity, where would they obtain it? And how, by what criterion shall we distinguish them from those that are not inborn? Critical consciousness finds with Locke that there are no innate ideas. After all: what else are innate ideas but ideas put into us by God? It is only a revival of the theory of revelation: rationalism saves itself through superreason, superrationalism.

After Descartes, Locke, Leibniz, after the sceptic Hume, comes the rationalist Kant with the thesis of a priori objects of knowledge which do not come from experience but from pure reason. You know how Kant produced a whole system out of such concepts of pure reason: the a priori forms of knowledge—time and space, the categories, or the most general concepts, like the notion of quantity, and causality, then the a priori ideas—soul, world, God, and for ethics the categorical imperative. An a priori concept one can recognize, he says because it is inevitable and general, whereas experience, sense, and ordinary reflection, "discoursive," not "intuitive," only provide accidental and particular concepts. A priori concepts are not innate, they are the "acts" of pure thought; they do not come from ourselves, they are notions begotten by pure reason without fertilization by experience, in fact something like an immaculate conception of spotless, unalloyed, pure reason—again a revelation, but a blind one.

One cannot accept Kant's a priorism. Already, if you please, that Kant makes a difference between "Verstand," and "Vernunft," and that this Vernunft is higher than Verstand; this is what the German language led him to. A Czech, and others besides, who have only one reason would not arrive at this epistemological dualism. It is one of Kant's great weaknesses that he did not produce a safe criterion for a priori concepts; he says that they are necessary, and universal: a very unreliable and uncertain criterion, for we draw many universal judgements also from experience, and that necessity is equally unreliable. When I am dealing with fundamental arithmetical and geometrical concepts, then I see the rightness and necessity of every mathematical theorem from the concepts themselves; mathematics, therefore, beginning with Pythagoras and Plato down to Kant and later, has been the model for certain knowledge, and the standard for the certainty of the other sciences. Kant also stuck to the model and, in fact, to the mathematical superstitition; by his a priorism, after this model, he tried to make natural sciences, and metaphysics, also certain besides mathematics. That was a mistake; after all, it is obvious that mathematical concepts are quite different from those of the natural sciences, and of metaphysics; the certainty of the natural sciences is different, being based more on experience than mathematical certainty.

But Kant's epistemology has yet another fatal weakness. For it makes a distinction between the thing in itself and the "world of appearances"; but where does such a difference arise? It can, in the extreme case, mean that man does not apprehend the real kernel, the real and inner substance of things, that he apprehends things only in part, approximately. There is sense in that, and it has been accepted from the very beginnings of more exact thought. But from the contrast between what appears to us, and the things as they really are, Kant created a sharp dualism: categories, and concepts a priori in general, particularly the category of causality, are valid only for phenomena, not for the things in themselves—how then does Kant know that there are any things in themselves, when the causal law is not valid for them, but only for phenomena? The thing in itself then cannot act on the subject if the law of causality is only valid for phenomena!

There would still be plenty of objections to Kant's a priorism; in addition to others there is also the one that objects of knowledge stated by Kant to be a priori can quite well be explained by experience, for instance, the intuitive forms of space and time, similarly, categories and ideas, like the idea of God, and some others.

Kant is the typical representative of a period of transition, of the transition from mythical revelation to critical, scientific empiricism. He sat on two stools—a theological and a philosophical one, —and by this very half-heartedness he achieved his reputation. He avoided extreme and non-sensical subjectivism—solipsism—by his metaphysical trick of "the thing in itself." Kant's followers, and German philosophy as a whole, did come to that extreme subjectivism; Fichte replaces Kant's "half-heartedness" by "absolute idealism," that is by solipsism, Schelling, directly and expressly, returns to myth, Schopenhauer made the world the work of our will and of our ideas. Instead of "absolute" idealism Hegel put his "objective" idealism—again another play with words; the absolute subject was re-christened the "objective spirit"—the deuce like the devil.

All Kant's a priorism is phantasy, myth; that dualism of pure and impure reason is the old dualism of reason and the senses based on the wrong psychological analysis of the process of perception. This contradiction between reason and the senses has been hanging over from the Greeks through the Middle Ages up to the present time. There is reason, and there are the senses, but they are not in conflict. I ask you, why should pure reason give better and more certain knowledge than impure reason which is connected with the senses, and which forms our experience?

8. *Epistemological Scepticism*

In opposition to all the theories concerning
nonempirical, superempirical, and therefore certain knowledge, Hume brought forward his scepticism; in so doing he placed the human mind
radically back within the limitations of uncertain
experience. It is a healthy scepticism, but scepticism all the same; and here it is to Kant's credit
that against scepticism he brought forward
criticism. Not scepticism, but criticism; not
to doubt, but to ascertain exactly, patiently,
critically.

Hume concentrated his scepticism on the
problem of causality; the concept of causality for
him is an empirical one, altogether all our per-
ceptions, except the mathematical ones, come
from experience, they are, therefore, inexact, and
uncertain; for that reason the metaphysical and
theological views concerning God, and similar
beings, are erroneous because they transgress
experience. The causal concept is not one of
reason, it is established by mere habit: man sees
the sun rise in the morning, he gets used to it,
and therefore expects it also to rise tomorrow.
Hume asserts that the concept of cause and effect
has its origin only in the association of ideas, thus
in the common experience that after A comes B.

So for Hume the whole of natural science is based on the blind concept of causality, it has no logical justification, it only rests on usage, on the psychological, not logical association of cause with effect. Certain knowledge only mathematics provides.

Against Hume's scepticism which rejected all knowledge as being uncertain except that of mathematics, which rejected not only metaphysics —not to speak of theology—but also empirical knowledge, appertaining to natural sciences— against this scepticism Kant brought forward his system of a priori concepts. By this a priorism he tried to guarantee the certainty of the findings of natural science, but also those of metaphysics, ethics and religion. He followed Hume in the idea that empirical knowledge is unreliable; in that way he hit upon the idea that the foundations of knowledge, that the fundamental concepts are supra-empirical, a priori, that causality, time, space, and what not are a priori—so that by those a priori concepts he might prop up empirical knowledge! Vain labour: that a priorism was a failure, it was a phantasy that took its revenge on its originator. Kant himself said that he "had to abolish knowledge to make room for faith". In the same way Comte developing Hume's positivism came eventually to fetishism. That is the fate of scepticism: that at last it tries to escape from itself—by plunging into phantasy.

Scepticism is possible in theory; but is consistent scepticism possible in practice?

Hardly—in so far as we are not mere onlookers, and critics of life. A sceptic in practice simply behaves like non-sceptics. There is no sceptical action, there is only sceptical thought. And what refers to epistemological scepticism—the fact that our concepts in natural sciences and in philosophy are only more or less probable—is no reason for scepticism. It is understood, empiricism, the experience of the senses is inaccurate, and unreliable; but it is controlled and developed by reason, even by exact mathematical reason as you see in modern natural science which is always becoming more and more applied mathematics.

It is important that Hume with his scepticism acknowledged the moral liability because its foundation, sympathy humanity is sanctioned by itself; to love one's neighbour, and because of that to help him as far as possible, that needs no proof that it is right—the sanction of sympathy is given by itself. That is right, and it is the more important that this doctrine comes from a sceptic. My first university lecture in Prague was on Hume's scepticism; in it already then I gave expression to my anti-sceptical programme. But for myself I can say: Hume was particularly important for me, he corrected what was of a Platonist in me; I should say the same for Marx's materialism.

9. Conclusions: Concretism

This already is characteristic of your own view.

Yes. Concretism in one word, is the opposite to scepticism; it recognizes not only reason but also the senses, the feelings, and the will, taken altogether, the whole experience of our consciousness; sticking to experience it rejects all non-empirical, contra - empirical, supra - empirical theories.

And so to a great extent: James's radical empiricism.

But without exceptional experiences. Scientific thought manages without them, except to examine them critically. Concretism above all is critical: it subjects experience to reason.

Concretism does not set senses and reason in opposition, it does not oppose reason to the other spiritual activities, it accepts man in his entirety; it acknowledges the substance and the value of all spiritual capacities and activities, it tries to find a rule for a full and harmonious life.

Concretism recognizes individualities in nature, in society, and in the whole world, and these it strives to know; it is fully aware that it obtains knowledge of particulars by abstract concepts.

For scientific interpretation concretism has this chief rule: to grasp things and explain them of themselves, not by the analogical method of myth. As far as is possible it replaces myth by critical, scientific knowledge. It strives for lucidity and exactness, it knows what it does know, and what it does not.

In addition to mathematical concepts it recognizes as well the concepts of natural science, of psychology, history, and of all other sciences as a whole. And the sciences—they are the experiences and reason of many individuals and of all ages. I verify my experiences and my reasoning by the reason and experience of others—other men also have reason and experience. All the time to bring to consciousness what we know, and what we don't know! Criticism, sir, must also be self-criticism. If we desire to achieve certainty for our knowledge there is only one way: scientific honesty, patience, and clarity; and then to offer one's concepts to the future generations for criticism and improvement. In all this concretism finds sufficient guarantees of truth.

Clear thinking is painful—the loss of myth is painful, often to understand new things is painful; there is also an epistemological xenophobia

—I deduce not only from ξένος, stranger, but also from τὸ ξένον, a strange and unknown thing; in thinking man is also a person of habit. Real wisdom, real knowledge is eternally young, eternally on the move, and new—then experience also is eternally new for us: "herrlich wie am ersten Tag," I should say with Goethe. Are you satisfied?

Yes. I suppose that your epistemological concretism has its complement in your Concrete Logic.

Yes. Epistemology investigates the substance and the rules of knowledge, concrete logic investigates knowledge in concreto, science, the system of science. I am working now on the second edition of my Concrete Logic—since the first edition in these last fifty years how tremendously have all the sciences extended and become specialized! I must find my bearings in them anew—that means work, sir, work, and gratifying work—if only one had more time!

And still another question. You yourself call your philosophy concretism; but people used to call you a positivist, or realist.

A positivist—no; but a realist yes, in philosophy and in politics. I ask you, they once reproached me for my mysticism—when I tried to prove to our liberals that religion is not something that is finished with. I could not simply and I cannot strike religion out of culture, particularly not out of our national culture. I think that my concretism is rational enough, but I do not see the fullness of spiritual life, and of endeavour solely in reason, I see it also in feeling, and will. The point is to harmonize the entire and full spiritual life of man —and of the nation. Our nation was strongly religious; take Saint Venceslas, Hus, Chelčický, Komenský! But equally strongly it aspired to knowledge. Komenský showed us the way to seek and find the harmony in all spiritual life, how to find, according to his words, THE DEPTH OF SECURITY. For this harmony in the field of knowledge concretism also strives. That is all.

II

METAPHYSICS

1. Knowledge and the World

AND now, please, a step from epistemology to metaphysics: does any objective reality correspond to our subjective experience to our knowledge?

Metaphysics—I don't like that word, apparently because I am such an unbending empiricist and practical man. In metaphysics men seek God knows what deep and mysterious knowledge, and in the meantime metaphysics, at least in the way that it has been developed up till now, is poor in content, very poor; it is merely a small competitive enterprise that philosophy set up in opposition to theology.

You were right, I should say, when you burst the door right open into the room; we are always back at the problem: subject—object. Epistemology and metaphysics belong to each other; knowledge demands something that is being apprehended, the one without the other is impossible.

Now when we have done with epistemology I can say: concretism is objective. We are against

59

subjectivism; extreme subjectivism, solipsism, which regards the world as our idea, and a mere product of our consciousness, is nonsensical. I ask you, if the world were our idea, if it were formed according to our reason and will, what would it look like!

But metaphysical dualism—not that. In abstracto, but only in abstracto ad usum of the logical dolphin we can talk of subject and object; in reality I am not alone, I am, you, we, there are innumerable subjects, and innumerable objects. I too am an object—to myself and to others.

Then your concretism is a kind of pluralism.

Yes. Concretism is pluralistic. It accepts the objective world, including the knowing subject; it accepts then the spiritual and the material world as an objective reality—and both worlds in the whole concrete plurality of all individuals. Men do not really doubt the material world—

I am just thinking to myself: if those little women over there from Topolčiany were to rake with an apparent rake the apparent sand on paths that are only in my mind—that they would leave it alone.

I don't know if a radical subjectivist would admit that argument. But the truth is that even the most intractable subjectivist forgets his subjectivism as soon as he sits down to his dinner. We accept the outward, objective world as the most reasonable hypothesis by which the world, and the subject itself can be most easily explained. We accept it, of course, critically.

There is a difference between objectivism —what is also called realism—naïve, the realism of an ordinary, unphilosophical man, and critical realism. A simple man is dead certain of the existence of everything he sees, hears, and so on. As soon as he begins to think, he perceives that the world is not quite the same as he imagined. He says to himself: was Plato, and after him those right down to Berkeley, Kant, and the post-Kantians, were those philosophical subjectivities only groping? Isn't there a speck of truth in them? That dead certainty recedes before criticism, and the philosopher says then to himself that besides various hypotheses of a more or less radical subjectivism, there is also that of critical realism.

I said — pluralism. Pluralism accepts the material world, even if it is not quite the same as it appears to us; it accepts also the spiritual world, the inner world of personal consciousness, and of innumerable consciousnesses, it accepts the world of souls, it accepts God. I am not a materialist, I am not a monist, I am not a pantheist or panentheist, I am not a dualist. I am a pluralist, the all is for me a harmonious system.

In this way I have poured out to you the whole of my metaphysics at one go.

2. Sub Specie Aeterni

A theist then; you accept theism—through what? Through feeling? Reason? Faith?

Through reason; what role faith has in it, that already is one of the problems of religion. I accept theism through experience and reason. The reasons and proofs of theism give me reason.

What proofs?

Mainly the teleological proof. The purposiveness of the world, of life, of historical happenings, of our knowledge, and of moral endeavour lead me to acknowledge a creator, and director of all, a personal being, spiritual, and infinitely perfect. God himself is reason, is νοῦς, λόγος. The Greeks understood this already when they freed themselves from mythological polytheism and fetishism; "reason," said Anaxagoras, "is an organizer of the cosmos," and Aristotle praised him for that because "he came like one sober among the drunk."

And how would you demonstrate that purposiveness?

By experience and reason. True, most people

only half-believe in purposiveness, and rather unconsciously. A man who would completely deny the order in the world, with its consequences, and the purpose of everything, even of his own life—I ask you, how could he exist with such an idea. Reason after all itself ascertains, and to a certain extent it also constructs an intelligent order in everything it conceives; reason already from its nature seeks for order and purpose, it itself formulates aims; to speak of chance, and aimlessness in the world is contrary to reason, reason itself is the agent of order and of teleology. A purposeful order in the world is provided by reason, our knowledge itself is teleological.

And how do you explain, whence, why, and what for is all evil, pain, and misery, wars, and catastrophes?

I shall not explain that, I cannot explain it. But neither monism, nor pantheism, nor dualism, nor materialism, and no one can explain it any better; I stick to it because of all the possible hypotheses concerning the substance and the origin of the world it is the simplest. Tell me, why should the bad, painful, nonsensical, what life gives to us count for more than what is healthy, cheerful, and pleasant? There is more good in the order of the world; but man feels that evil is stronger. I cannot honestly explain what is served by imperfection, suffering and so on; but I see, that man and mankind can and should face the imperfections. Without the overcoming of obstacles, without pressing and sometimes even painful occasions for action life would not be a full life. I think that philosophy need not refute pessimism and justify God. God has no need of an advocate. And to refute pessimism? Illness, misery, crime, and so on cannot be refuted with words. Don't think that I should close my eyes to physical and spiritual incongruities and misery. When recently I visited Zidlichovice in Moravia I heard the nightingales singing there, well, beautifully! They told me that this year the nightingales were singing because they had plenty of mosquitos. And a thought passed through my mind: do those nightingales sing their praises to the Good Lord for those mosquitoes? And those mosquitoes—that buzzing of theirs, is that also a song of praise because the nightingales are swallowing them as they fly? Teleology—a hard nut, but even if you can't crack it, it is more likely to get into the palm of your hand than a theory of aimlessness, chance and chaos.

The second argument of theism, here we have the so-called cosmological proof: without a first cause, without a first creator, and mover we cannot understand the origin, motion, and development of the universe. From the causal point of view we must put some beginning to that chain of causes; it does not suffice for us, I think, to accept secondary causes in infinitum. And the positivistic ignoramus, the teaching of the impossibility of knowing the first causes, agnosticism in general, I do not regard as any explanation of the world and of life.

Even psychologically it is strange: not to allow oneself to enquire about first causes. It is like the fairy tale of the nine chambers. You are allowed to go into all the chambers except the tenth. Then one thinks that in those nine chambers there is nothing special, and that only the tenth is worth anything.

That's about it; and there's nothing more than that in it, nothing perhaps. Hume and Comte made a mistake when they rejected a limine all enquiry into causes——Comte prohibited it almost as the police might do; also it turned out with him as one would expect, he fell into myth up to his ears.

I think that modern natural science in its teaching of entropy confirms Aristotle s postulate of the first cause: if according to the mechanical theory of heat the universe ends with the same temperature in all its parts, and so with a heat death, then the world is not eternal but it had a beginning in time, and in time it also will have its end. I know that this explanation is not accepted by some physicists.

You deduce the existence of God by these two arguments alone?

Yes. More accurately speaking, the HYPOTHESIS of the existence of God; for science theism is a hypothesis which according to the demand of logic is simpler, and therefore more justifiable than other hypotheses, such as materialism and so on. I would go further; as a theist, as a pluralist, I also accept the existence of the soul and its immortality, I am certain of the soul, and of souls; but to prove that by intellectual arguments which would silence everybody—that I can't do. After all there are scientists who defend materialism, pantheism, monism, and so on—I don't regard myself as infallible, and as knowing everything better. I think that the hypothesis of an immortal soul is not in conflict with biology and psychology, it is not with science. At one time, when I was young, it upset me that I had no proofs that were absolutely invincible. Today I say to myself: must we, can we know everything, and have it down in legal black and white? What a world would it be if it had no secret for us! If we believed that we knew everything we should grow much too fat. When I was a schoolmaster and taught philosophy, the boys used to come to me, and ask about this and that; they could not understand when I used to say—I don't know. They were astonished at the kind of philosopher I was who had not an answer for everything.

But even if you can't prove the immortality of the soul, at least you must have reasons why you are certain of it.

That, yes! I cannot imagine that such a beautiful and fine feeling as thought, knowledge, piety, moral endeavour, perception of beauty, all culture, that it could go lost, that it could not be for something. The physicists say—energy is indestructible; and what about the energy in us? The soul moves the matter, reason gives form to the matter, determines the aim, and comprehends the whole of this world: can that matter last—and not the soul? It would be strange.

And then: life itself is an argument against death. It is true, all living things die; but all living things have a tremendous urge to live, to outlive themselves, to survive without change. A plant lives again in its offspring, hands on everything further, and loses nothing of its qualities. The soul alone would not inherit itself, the soul alone would have no continuation. That would be unnatural.

You might say—our deeds outlive us. But how many people are lucky enough to hand over any real achievement to the coming generations? Some die young, others are not given any opportunity for making use of their talents. I can't believe that that potential work in them can be lost just anyhow. It would be unjust.

We cannot prove the immortality of the soul; but on the other hand—we cannot really imagine not-being and not-life; we can only imagine the end of life in a negative sense: that we do not see, do not hear, do not know. Our concept of death is as empty as the concept of not-tree, or not-grass. Perhaps on account of that emptiness we fear death like a dark abyss.

It depends: I am not afraid of it, many people are not. Primitive races have no knowledge of the fear of death. People in the Middle Ages were not afraid of it—it is only modern man who is frightened of it. Above all things he is more afraid of pain than the men of old——

as the dying Wolker wrote: "I do not fear death, death is not bad, it is but the end of a hard life. It is dying that I fear."

And secondly—many a modern man is afraid of death because he is too self-indulgent—life is not for him a big drama, all he wants from it is food and pleasure; he is an unbeliever, he has not sufficient faith and trust. Modern suicide and fear of death—these two are connected together in the same way as fear and flight are connected. But that would be a problem in itself. When I think of immortality, I don't think so much of death, and what will come after, but rather of life and its content. For me, immortality follows from the richness and value of human life, of the human soul. Man to himself, man to man is most valuable as a spiritual being. And the immortality of the soul follows also from the acknowledgement of God, from faith in universal order and justice. There would be no justice, there would be no perfect equality without the eternity of the soul. And lastly—immortality is already experienced now, in this life; we have no experience of life after death, but we have, we can already have experience now, that the real, and fully human life we live is only sub specie aeterni. This experience ultimately depends upon us, on how we live, on what we are concerned with, and on what we try to make of our present lives. Only as souls among eternal souls do we live a full and true life. The existence of the soul is the real basis of democracy: the eternal to the eternal cannot be indifferent, one immortal is in equality with another immortal. This is where love of one's neighbour derives its special — it is usually called metaphysical — significance.

3. *The Soul and the World*

True, I cannot say what the soul is like and what it is; I ascribe spiritual activities to the soul and partly also to the body, the brain, the senses; but how the soul and the body act on each other, that I don't know—after all, no explanation, whether it be materialism or psychological parallelism can explain that satisfactorily. And what will it be like, what will life be like after death —that I know still less. I don't know how to believe that after death we shall pass into some divine primary substance as monism, pantheism teach: I want to be myself also after death, I don't want to dissolve into some metaphysical jelly; I am a metaphysical individualist if you like to call me that. Perhaps after death we shall be given fuller and more complete knowledge, also knowledge of God; it may be that life after death is an asymptote approaching to God: always and always nearer, eternally nearer—well yes, this also is a continuation of life upon earth, because God is the chief and foremost object of our thinking, knowing, and striving God and the soul. One is connected with the other. The Soul and God, that is the dual problem of our thinking, and striving—I should say, the true task of life.

METAPHYSICS

You talk like a pure spiritualist; and yet all your life you have been taking on other tasks, actual, practical, real ones—it is not for nothing that they called you a realist.

Of course, sir; but even in the actual and material, a spiritual and eternal process is taking place. Only today I found in my papers the oriental aphorism: "A man should act as if everything mattered, but in his inner self a small Buddha sits for whom nothing matters." Nothing—that is expressed and felt in the oriental way; in our way it would be; for whom behind all that is temporal, and material, what is eternal and spiritual matters. Faith in the spiritual, the accent on the spiritual, does not mean that we ought to, and are allowed to disregard matter and the body. After all in a philosophical sense, we do not know what the substance of matter is. It is given us like the soul, it is given to us only by way of the soul, through our perception and thinking: what right have we got to undervalue it? All knowledge of matter is only the expansion of our spiritual activities; soul and matter are not in opposition to each other. The soul, body, and matter, all reality is given to us for our knowledge, and development; our souls and our material surroundings we ought to develop to greater perfection. The idea that matter is something lower and less pure than the spirit is wrong. In this Plato went wrong, and after him the theologians and philosophers because with contempt they turned away from matter, nature, and the world.

And yet you call yourself a Platonist.

Yes. But that does not mean that I accept all Plato's views. I am a Platonist in so far as I seek ideas in the cosmos, that in what is transitory I seek what is enduring, and eternal. I cannot be interested solely in movement, but in WHAT is moving, WHAT is changing. In natural development I seek purpose and order, sense in historical progress; I enquire for what purpose it all happened, and where it is leading to. Against Darwinism, against one-sided evolutionism, and historicism, I accentuate the static side: that, that is permanent and eternal. Not simply the παντα ξει of Heraclitus, not simply continual change, but the substance of the things that change; in addition to dynamics, and with it statics, the great architecture of all being. In man, therefore, I also seek that which endures: his immortal soul.

4. *Providence*

To look for a purpose and meaning in events, and in history, that is almost like believing in Providence.

Of course. I do believe, I must believe in Providence which governs the development of the world, and of humanity, and of any one of us. Once I acknowledge God the creator, and director, I must see in everything some order, plan, and reasonable aim.

Or determinism.

Yes, that's understood. Determinism means a fixed order in Nature, in man, in society, and in its development: everywhere exact law. We find it in matter, we discover the beautiful order of the atoms; more and more we shall be able to see this obedience to law in the life of the man, in the history of states, nations, and of humanity, sir, and we shall be able to collaborate with it consciously! The more knowledge we shall acquire the clearer will the aim and purpose of everything be revealed to us; knowledge itself is the ascertainment of laws, and the bringing of facts into lawful order; and that is only the beginning.

When you say determinism you raise with it the old problem: what then happens with the freedom of the will. If our actions are directed, whether by Providence or by natural causation, is not our supposed will and moral freedom only an illusion?

It is not. We can choose—after all, experience itself guarantees us this. Only in the causal world can we anticipate, act with forethought, prepare

73

for the future, consistently, with real will. Determinism excludes not freedom, but caprice, fancy, and instability, it leads to perseverance, and consistency—without determinism, without the exact concatenation of cause and effect there would be no responsibility. There would be mere fortuity; we should not be responsible for our deeds, and the motives for our actions would rise up in us without reason by mere chance.

I think that freedom of the will is not an infringement of causality; it is only the possibility of putting new causes into the causal process.

I should say it like this: the freedom and predestination of man is given by his relation to God, omnipotent, and omniscient, knowing the past and the future, determining this future. Man is after the divine image, God could not create man except after the likeness of his own image; from this follows for man a conscious synergism collaboration, with the divine will. In acquiring knowledge of Nature, and of man, in revealing the natural laws, spiritual and historical, in accepting and fulfilling those laws we participate in the divine creation and direction of the world. God lets us do his work, He wants us to work, and so collaboration. Every co-operation, among men too, includes freedom and subjection, initiative and constraint. Synergism with the divine will gives gives man his measure of freedom and of determinism the stronger and the more conscious he is, the more of both.

Determinism—yes: people think that it deprives man of responsibility. But God does not command me to lift now my right hand, or now the left: minima non curat praetor. Along with God, and under God, we are autonomous beings; we have the right of initiative, and we bear also the burden of responsibility. Hence the duty of activism, and of striving, of resoluteness, and of courage. Freedom, sir, is just as hard as duty. We feel that to will hurts. To will is labour; to decide tires, it is the creation of something new. During the War I envied the soldiers, that they were ordered about, that they could only obey, and need not decide. I had to decide, to command even all the time, not only to think, but to will terribly—I know then what it is.

Determinism does not mean the absence of freedom, on the contrary. An immature man who does not understand the order of the world, and its grandeur, a man in his primeval weakness, and lack of judgement sees in the world, and also in his own life a kaleidoscope of single, unconnected phenomena, everywhere he sees the unreasonable caprice of spirits, gods, of chance, and of blind fate.

75

That can also be seen today: the superstitious most likely are those dependent on chance: gamblers, hunters, people from the theatre, and such like.

Naturally: those who believe in chance, believe also in idols, and in miracles. Superstition is indeterminist. A primitive man is a metaphysical indeterminist; he succumbs blindly to impulses, he lets himself be led by his own whims—he is a metaphysical anarchist.

I should not say that. As with savages, with natural races, the life of an individual is mainly bound by tradition, the prescriptions of ritual, and social customs.

So you see, an indeterminist is a slave: he is bound blindly by customs and superstitions, he is subject to instincts, he has no free will. There are also primitives like that among us. A man has only as much reasonable freedom, as much determinism as he can understand in himself and in the order of the world.

Those controversies over determinism and indeterminism—a curious history, as old as philosophical thought. Already with the Greeks the expression was used: δεος αναιτιος, God without blame. The minds of people in the Middle Ages were racked by predestination: if God knows and determines everything, he knows already, and predestines who is going to be good, who evil, who will be saved, and who damned. St. Paul, Augustine, Thomas Aquinas, and later Luther, Zwingli, and Calvin had strange views on pre-destination; they tried partly to alleviate the harsh-ness of predestination by the doctrine of divine grace. Modern theologians also often invent only words, not concepts, how to reconcile the freedom of the human will with divine omnipotence—it leads nowhere, it seems to me; I am not astonished that one pope simply banned all controversies about the freedom of the will and predestination. It is a hard nut.

To me determinism is a consequence of theism, of the acknowledgement of the teleological order in the world. We also are fulfilling universal laws and are acting causally.

Even in our mistakes?

Of course; but we have the possibility of choosing amidst the plurality of causes, it is possible for us to judge. All education, and re-education, moral responsibility, and punish-ment, is based on determinism. We hope that through education we may inculcate into children motives of good behaviour; and for what would punishment be if it did not deter, if it were not the cause and the motive of reform?

And what about capital punishment?

That is a chapter to itself. The right to punish

by death is dreadful, and judging from its history and development, it will be abolished in future. Don't you ask me how I felt when I signed the order for carrying out capital punishment. Capital punishment for me is not mainly requital, nor deterrent, it is no safeguard against a dangerous criminal; if it has any sense and justification then it is only as expiation. Nothing but death compensates for and redeems such a terrible thing as the brutal and mercenary murder of a man; a criminal like that has committed an offence against the whole of mankind. But this also is only valid for the existing state of culture—future ages will have greater possibilities of prevention, correction, and re-education—and a better knowledge of criminal responsibility.

In these and other problems progress will have to be by empirical methods: to try to explain how man really does act in particular circumstances; to what extent he can control himself, and his actions, and educate himself; how far he is free and responsible for his actions. I confess that I prefer conscientious statistics, of accidents, say, to a few chapters of Leibniz' *Theodicea;* from statistics I learn what generally is the cause of accidents, and how to deal with them accordingly. If the driver does not drink mishaps do not happen so easily—ergo don't drink, and that's the end of it, and don't you try to blame, or justify the Good Lord. Illness—for that there are doctors, and science, so that they learn how to face them. Misery—we are all here to remove that. And so on.

This then is determinism: to learn to understand the causes of evil, so that we may induce the causes of reform. Not to be a fatalist, or a slave, a slave of oneself, or a slave of one's surroundings. Wherever we are, not to act and work blindly, but freely and consciously, to anticipate and plan like a worker and collaborator of God. In this I also differ from stoicism. Stoicism makes a virtue out of weakness, it is, if I may call it, a metaphysical shrugging of the shoulders, in it there is a suspicion of titanic dissimulation; theistic resignation is hopeful modesty.

III

RELIGION

1. *On Religion*

YOU brought forward arguments for theism. But however good they are, arguments are not enough for one to build a religion on.

That's understood; theism and religion are not the same. For philosophy and science theism is a hypothesis for the explanation of the origin and evolution of the world; and there are other hypotheses besides. For a man who thinks scientifically theism becomes religion when it is a conscious, emotional, personal relation of man to God, and through God to one's neighbour and to the world. To a religious man God is a central idea in thought and in action.

In the philosophy of religion I am an exponent of concretism, a realist: I observe various religions everywhere in the world, I study them, and as far as possible I compare them with the religion of the Christian churches; these I know best, and I myself have grown up in them in a religious sense. I have waded through all possible theories of religion, through the works of theologians and of scientists. Even in childhood I racked my brains wondering how it is that there are different Christian faiths, and I tried to compare them—this interest has never left me right up to the present day. I remember when I was a little scholar how upset I was by a calendar in which I read of the Russian Church, and that in it there are many saints and miracles; hadn't I heard from infancy that except for the Catholic Church all other confessions were false? It puzzled and excited me tremendously.

Would you have this interest in religion if you yourself were not a believer?

Certainly I should, but not so strong; after all, it is a big thing that there are religions, with their institutions all over the world, and in all ages; when in every village I see a church surpassing in beauty and size the dwellings of man, how can one not see it, and not think about it? How those village steeples and perhaps only turrets, point up to the sky? And our Prague—is it not one of a hundred towers? The Prague of a hundred towers, that means a religious Prague, doesn't it?

Well then, the theory of religion. By the word religion we mean all manifestations of religiousness; without religiousness there is no religion—except for registration. Religiousness then is a conscious and acknowledged relation towards God, the deity; this relation is also expressed in the various views on religion, in divine services, and so on.

But religiousness is a subjective factor, purely personal; while religion nearly always transgresses the sphere of one's personal relation to God.

I know. Religion as we see it in reality is, as a rule, collective, communal, national; it is codified in impersonal dogmas, and it is organized into churches; it changes, it preserves within itself survivals from the past, frequently extending back to primitive times, it develops and becomes more perfect with the development of thought and culture. Religion is a formation that is tremendously composite, stretching out in many directions: that is why a careful analysis is required of its elements, components, manifestations, or what should I call them. Wait, I will bring it for you tomorrow written down on a bit of paper, so that I shall not forget anything important.

How could religion help being complex! It gets hold of the whole man, his mind, his feelings and actions, his whole life; it gets hold of nations and of all society: all culture can be religious, as we see with the Greeks and the Romans, and most clearly in the Middle Ages. Nothing is so creative, nothing so all-embracing as religion.

RELIGION

2. *The Analysis of Religion*

Well, I have written down here some points about religion, what it is, how it manifests itself.

1. The substance of religion is theism, the acknowledgement of the existence of God, the certainty that God is, God omnipotent, creator and director of the universe.

2. Religion is a faith, believing, not-doubting; from a psychological standpoint faith is a judgement, conviction, general proposition; religious faith is a proposition of divinity, thus of a being inaccessible to the senses, but in which we firmly "believe."

3. Religions have their creeds, doctrines, dogmas, commandments.

4. Associated with theism as a rule is faith in personal immortality, in an immortal and spiritual soul.

5. With theism and faith in immortality, one meets with faith in things transcendental in a wider compass—faith in angels, saints, spirits, devils, and so on, in the "other" world as a whole. Theism, that is monotheism, gradually developed out of polytheism and lower forms of religion.

6. Positive religion, as one calls it, refers to revelation as the source of all religious doctrines and institutions: namely that the divinity revealed

itself to man, and manifested to him its will by direct communication, inspiration, or command. There are various forms of revelation: the deity speaks, makes signs, appears in dreams and so on. Revelation par excellence is the Christian faith that God took on man's flesh in order to reveal himself to man; Jesus not only taught, but also as an example lived and dwelt in this world among men, and for men, for many years.

People accept revelation with their senses and reason but it is above reason and against reason. Therefore: credo quia absurdum est.

7. Revelation has a wider conception in the Christian faith; that is to say various transcendental beings appear, like angels, saints, and the spirits of the departed, and the devil too. To a polytheist various gods and idols appear.

8. Mysticism is a special form of revelation: a mystic believes himself to be in direct union with the deity; God does not appear to him merely objectively, but subjectively, he receives Him somehow in himself, in various degrees of ecstasy. Mysticism is conceived as spiritual gazing, not with the eyes, but spiritually, with the soul.

9. Religious knowledge—in addition to faith in what is revealed—is often referred to as intuition, knowledge through feeling, non-sensual, non-intellectual knowledge.

10. Religious transcendentalism leads to the mysterious, to what is recondite, to what is secret.

11. This peculiarity of religious knowledge and feeling, and its mystery, leads to the use of symbols in theology and in divine service.

12. Religious faith is authoritative: the highest authority—the deity—determines religious truth; therefore the authority of tradition, and of the general consensus is acknowledged: quod semper, quod unique, quod ab omnibus creditum est. God and his revelation appear to be the same for ever, even if one admits that revelation took place bit by bit, in various epochs. Every man must accept revealed truth in the form in which it is revealed and handed down.

Religion being by its essence authoritative, is objective. Theism is against extreme religious subjectivism.

13. Religion is not only believing and knowing but also divine service. Divine service consists of various ceremonies, especially prayer and sacrifice. Divine service as a unique performance, solemn and supremely important, is performed in places specially sought out in Nature, and in special buildings, churches, temples.

Prayer is also divine service, but private. Real prayer is raising one's mind to God. Jesus pointed out that God knows the needs of men; He does not require any information about them. Most people pray that God might do something impossible for them, they beg for a miracle.

14. The miraculous in almost every religion is a very important element. The godhead is raised immensely high above man, it is the creative director of the universe, it can do anything; hope and gratitude are considerable subjective elements in every religion.

This natural urge for the miraculous sees in miracles actual material revelation. On a lower plane of culture besides spirits and idols there are sacred objects, sanctified material, resort to which assists man in his misery: sacraments, amulets, and charms. Miraculous powers are also sought from saints and spirits; from faith in saints and their miraculous powers it is only a step to the invocation of evil spirits, of the devil.

Superstition readily becomes associated with faith; as the word suggests[1] it is also faith, as a skeleton key is also a key. Superstition is faith turned upside down, a superstitious thief and a murderer makes an offering of prayers so that he may succeed in his crime.

15. Religion is not only a theoretical but mostly a practical affair of mankind; possessing divine

[1] In Czech pověra means superstition, víra or věra means faith, páklíč means a skeleton key, while klič means a key.

authority it determines morality. On the higher plane morality becomes an important part of religion: for Jesus the substance of religion is comprised in the love of God and of one's neighbour. With cultural development morality overshadows the cult, but to many the cult is still above morality.

16. In intimate relation to religion is all art: architecture, sculpture, painting, music, poetry, rhetoric, rhythmics; already with the Greeks, and long before them, in addition to mythology and philosophy art expressed and formulated religious ideas and feelings; a strong artistic element is present in religious ceremonies. The Catholic mass, for instance, is clearly an all-comprehensive work of art.

The inner relationship of art to religion lies in the fact that art is creative; the Greeks called a poet a creator—in art one also sees revelation, and the artist's aesthetic exaltation is similar to religious exaltation.

17. Religion is practical, vital in a true sense of the word. It is not defined clearly enough by its dogmas, or ceremonies, or by its history, but by the understanding of its substance, and this is the consciousness of the dependence of man upon the deity, upon God; this means the bringing into consciousness of human frailties, physical,

spiritual, and moral—bringing them into consciousness, and overcoming them at the same time. For religion is trust and hope; hopefulness is the substance of religion. A religious man in his weakness desires miracles and a Saviour. It takes a long time for him to become without religious fear. In the older religions, even in the Old Testament, religion is fear, terror before the deity; God, Jehovah, is terrible; in Jesus' teaching there is no longer any fear.

Religion is the orientation of man to the universe, to God, to the world, and to himself: it is not only the comprehension but the evaluation of the world and of life. It is not only the understanding of the sense of life as a whole, it is at the same time a state of mind springing from this understanding of life and of the world.

Life is lived: in religion man obtains the deepest sense of his life.

Religion, religiousness is a purely human affair; God is not religious. Man—God are two poles of human life, and of the world given to man.

18. Religion brings people together; every faith, every conviction unites the believers into a society; the churches are religious social organizations.

The churches as a rule are organized by a special clerical rank, by priests, preachers along with the laymen, and above them; the priests are the guardians of the mystery, the performers of the ceremonies, the organs and representatives of the deity.

Besides the ordinary theologians the churches have their special prominent teachers, so to speak, their professional authorities in religion.

The prophets form a class by themselves—the religious geniuses, more like zealots than prophets; authority that is quite unique is exercised by the founders of religion, like Moses, Jesus, Mohammed, and the reformers.

The authoritativeness of religion naturally passes over on to the churches and its organs.

19. Just as religion and church determine the relation of man to his neighbour and to society, they also determine his relation to all social organizations, especially towards the state.

Churches are necessarily in close relation to the state; and this partly on religious, partly on moral grounds, as long as the state also bases its administration—laws, and so on—and politics on morality. There are various forms of the special relation between the church and the state: various forms of theocracy; in the course of time particularly in democracies, and in republics, separation of the church and state takes place to a greater or less extent.

As well as the state, and together with it,

society is also organized according to nationality; therefore the relation of religion and of the church to nationality is another serious problem, especially in modern times, when nationality apart from the state has assumed a significance that did not exist in the Middle Ages, and in Antiquity, national churches are arising.

20. For religion as for all other manifestations of the human spirit and of its life's endeavour, there is a special science—theology.

Theology developed along with religion and culture in general.

It is no accident that a systematic theology was worked out by Aristotle for the first time as the chief part of his metaphysics; "theologians" before Aristotle was the name for the thinkers who occupied themselves with thinking about the deities and with the transcendental as a whole.

In the Middle Ages theology was the chief and all-embracing science; theology, of course, ecclesiastical, christian, catholic; apart from it philosophy was cultivated, but as ancilla theologiae.

The modern period, when compared with the Middle Ages, is characterized on one side by the religious reformation, and new Protestant churches, on the other by the strengthening and renaissance of ancient philosophy and art, at the same time by the establishment of the sciences, and in this way by making philosophy scientific. Thus in addition to the medieval ecclesiastical theology, and in opposition to it, the new philosophy and science appropriated ex thesi the casting vote in all truth. The conflict arises between philosophy and science on the one side, and theology and ecclesiastical religion on the other. This conflict is an ancient one, and it arises from the natural criticism of thoughtful men; it revealed itself already with the Greeks and the Romans, in modern times it is more general, and mainly deeper.

21. Religion arrogating to itself the will and decree of the highest authority, the deity itself, regards itself as absolute, as absolutely right and truthful, as infallible. Not Catholicism alone, please; but Catholicism attributes infallibility to the pope, the Protestants to the Bible, or church —yes, even to the state.

With religious, in actual fact, priestly or ecclesiastical infallibility, we still meet with intolerance, and aggressiveness in the churches. From that again aversion arises to the ecclesiastical religion, the authoritative one.

22. So already a long time ago—see in Paul! —in opposition to the positive religion, revealed, ecclesiastical, authoritative, stood perhaps from the very beginning of human thought the natural

religion, the postulate, that religion and theology should not be contrary to reason, science, philosophy. Theology must not conflict with scientific philosophy; we see in fact how philosophy always worked its way into theology; this is most obvious in the development of theology from the Middle Ages down to the present day.

I have explained the epistemological difference between myth and science, and the conflict between the cult of myth and the cult of science; man immersed in myth conceives of religion as a myth; his theology is mythical; the thinking man, proceeding critically and scientifically, has a scientific theology, a philosophical one. To the present day theology is the organ of myth, while philosophy becomes the organ of science. This means a long-standing conflict between theology and philosophy; it is also—inaccurately—presented as a conflict between religion and science.

23. With religion the problem of irreligion and non-religiousness, heresy and heterodoxy arises. Thence come ecclesiastical apologetics and polemics, thence also ecclesiastical philosophy, as the ancilla theologiae striving to support religious doctrine by intellectual reasons.

24. Religion today is also the object of scientific investigation: a special philosophy of religion has arisen which tries to elucidate scientifically

the whole substance of religion; the psychology of religion analyses religious life, and experience; religion is further studied sociologically and historically. We have the history of the religious development of individual nations, numerous attempts are made to comprehend the religion of primitive races. The religious life of certain classes and ranks, of the town and of the country, is investigated, and so on.

Of course: it is something different to think objectively about religion, about the various religions as we find them everywhere in the world, about the various religious ideas, doctrines, and institutions, to analyse them, compare them, to trace their development; and quite another thing to be religious, to have one's own religious credo, one's personal creed, to realize how it differs from non-faith, or another faith.

3. *The Religion of Jesus*

Well—this is about the essence of my philosophy of religion; of course, those twenty-four small paragraphs are only a short summary of various monographs on religion. Many believers do not know what religion is, many unbelievers have no real idea of what they are denying; but

93

least, and most superficially, do indifferent and indolent people understand religion. To get them to a state so that at least they would think about religion—that, sir, would be a great missionary work, more essential than going to preach to the negroes, who believe according to their lights, but they do believe. Today there is a need of missionaries for the intelligentsia—of course, intelligent ones, and genuinely religious.

I have noticed one: whenever you mention your own faith you quote Christ and the Apostles.

Yes. Jesus—I usually do not say Christ—for me he is the example and teacher of religiousness; he teaches that love towards a kind God, love of one's neighbour and even of one's enemy, and thus a pure, unstained humanity, is the substance of religion. Religiousness and morality for Jesus are the chief elements of religion. Notice that in the Gospels—in comparison with the Old Testament, or with Greek mythology—there is almost no mythology, almost no cosmology, and eschatology, almost no history; there you do not find detailed regulations concerning cult and ritual; nor ecclesiastical organization. Jesus gives almost nothing but moral instructions, he turns continually to practical questions as he is forced by the life around him; he manifests himself his love towards his neighbour by effective help in

spiritual and physical misery. Just look again
into the Gospels: how discreet are Jesus' theological prescriptions, and his references to the
transcendental! God is father to him, to Him he
is in an intimate personal relation, but he does
not speak of this relation much, he lives it, and
he does not lay down any system of theology.
Jesus was a living example; he did not preach
love merely with words, but he continually put
it into practice, he associated with the poor, and
lowly, he sought out the sinners, and those
morally outcast, he healed the sick, filled the
hungry, he warned the rich. Such a living faith
spreads more by example than with words, like
a fire, like an infection. Jesus gave no proof of
his religion, speaking always as one that had
authority; he entered into no theological disputes,
but he confuted the Scribes and Pharisees by
pointing to the falseness of their religiousness and
morality. He showed that real religion, real
religiousness permeates the whole of life, even
the daily one, the ordinary one, and it permeates
it always, at every moment; most people are
satisfied with Sabbath-day religion, with an
ostentatious, and hardly sincere religion—only
in exceptional circumstances, especially when
things are looking bad, do they remember the
Good Lord, and cry for help and expect signs

and miracles. But eternal life will not be only after death, and in the other world—we live in eternity already now, and always. Of course, people do not like to be aware of that, they put eternity a long way from them; they keep it in reserve for the time after death. Religion can be experienced not only in church, but also in the factory, in the field, in the cowshed, and in the drawing-room, in sadness, and in joy. That is Jesus' example.

And do you accept the historical person of Jesus?

In the Gospels, in the old Christian literature as a whole, and in tradition, the rich and homogeneous personality of Jesus emerges; that, sir, is difficult to think out, and put together merely from a series of legends. For me the Gospels, and the old Christian literature are enough; thei contents give a plastic, lively, and fine picture of the beginnings and development of Christianity, of its doctrine, of the people and of the church, nd for me that seems to be the chief thing. Above all things the quality of the doctrine, and the character of the personality to whom this doctrine is ascribed are the things that count. The doctrine and the personality are unique, tremendous.

The personality is so lifelike that one is tempted to follow it further.

I have read the most important so-called biographies of Jesus; in none of them do I find so much religious life as in the Gospels. The Gospels have the very smell of reality. It is impossible to write the real life of Jesus, there are too many accounts: from Jesus himself we have not a word that is genuinely authentic, he himself wrote and left nothing. The first accounts come from Paul who died, I believe, about the year 64, and the Gospels were written from about the year 70 onwards. Also the text of the whole New Testament that has come down to us is open to doubt in many and important parts, there have been interpolations, mistakes in copying, mistakes in translation, and so on; but the main doctrine and religious character of Jesus is caught by the Scriptures well and clearly enough.

And what about the other religious geniuses, say Buddha, Lao-Tse. . . .

I do not presume to pass judgement of them, I have not concerned myself with them very much, but this at least I am prepared to say: They do not overshadow Jesus. If some modern Europeans seek in them a religion higher than that of Jesus it is, I think, due to cultural weariness; they need something exotic to excite their jaded religious phantasy. In that as well the modern crisis in religion stands revealed. I have a special appreciation for the oriental wisdom of resignation, but the wisdom of effective love is much higher.

4. *The Religion of Love*

Your religion appears to be based more on love towards your neighbour than on the hypothesis of God.

Not that. Love of one's neighbour, the moral law of love is for me only a prominent and practical manifestation of religion. Religion, religiousness is, as I have said, a standpoint, an attitude towards the universe, towards everything that is given to us, and so towards God, the world, towards mankind and towards ourselves.

In actual life the relation of man to man is most important. A man towards man has inborn love, sympathy, a feeling of companionship and humanity; this feeling is its own justification, it cannot, and need not be proved, it need not be explained, it simply is. But it can be strengthened, deepened, refined; religion, chiefly Jesus' religion, is a culture of love. Religion binds man to man not only with natural sympathy but with that common attitude towards God, life, the world, or as one says to destiny.

It seems to me that that inborn and self-evident

love towards one's neighbour would also persist without religion, without faith.

True, but not in its fullness. Religiousness crowns and sanctifies love. Religion without humanity cannot be true; humanity without religiousness cannot be complete. John says: "If a man say, I love God, and hateth his brother, he is a liar: for he that loveth not his brother whom he hath seen, how can he love God whom he hath not seen?"

Jesus' commandment of love towards one's neighbour is sufficient for dealings between man and man; Paul already correctly deduced all the prohibitions of the Ten Commandments from the humanitarian commandment.

Jesus's commandment also includes and prescribes love towards oneself: not egoism, but conscious care of oneself, of the salvation of one's soul. We are with ourselves all the time, we can be influencing ourselves all the time, even if it is often more difficult than to influence others; therefore we ought to care for ourselves, so that others need not care for us. Jesus expressed that nicely and practically: love your neighbour as yourself; so care for yourself, learn to know yourself, respect yourself, be sincere to yourself, and truthful, and don't annoy others. Always be prepared, alert, be active, determined, have courage, and don't run away from responsibility.

Love, true love is activity, work, collaboration, creation for others and for oneself. It is not sentimental—sentimentality is egoistic, and indulges in its own feelings.

Love of one's neighbour is not only compassion in misfortune, it is not only commiseration, it is also shared pleasure.

Love of one's neighbour is in the scheme of the world, human society rests on love; but it is not enough to have towards fellow beings only the so-called kindly feeling—love, humanity must express itself in work, in collaboration, in creation, and by this in the perfecting of the world that is given to us. We are workers in the divine vineyard.

Effective love presupposes knowledge of one's neighbours, and of oneself, so that one may notice what a person is needing. To know oneself, to be severe with oneself, to be modest; that is why one speaks of Christian humility. Love makes us practical—religiousness does not want muddlers. Even in the Gospels regret is expressed that the children of light often are not so wise as the children of this world. Jesus says, be like doves, and like serpents—a wise forbearance is necessary but also ingeniousness, practicality and cleverness.

This love, of course, also existed before Jesus.

But it was Jesus who consummated it; he came "to fulfil the law," also that universal and eternal law of love. The historical act of Jesus consisted in the fact that he was the first clearly and by his own example to define religiousness not only as a relation towards God, but also to one's neighbour. Before Jesus religion used to be, and also after him it is often enough unkind, inhuman, harsh; take the cruelties that the Jews of the Old Testament committed in the name of what, according to them, was the true God! Similarly the Mohammedans. But the Christians as well, although they had the gospel of love they spread their faith with fire and sword, they devised the Inquisition, and taught people to hate those who held other beliefs. Inhumanity, and cruelty are the fruit of a slavish mind, of the slaves and slave-drivers together; slavery and slave-drivers affect each other. There can be no humanity without mutual trust, a religious man is not frightened of another man. The same John already knew that: "There is no fear in love; but perfect love casteth out fear; because fear hath torment. He that feareth is not made perfect in love." A religious man is strong.

Xenophobia, intolerance, and fanaticism are not compatible with true religiousness; there is not only a national and political chauvinism, but also a religious, social, and cultural one—in all spheres of activity intolerance and standoffishness makes it impossible for men to live together peaceably, and collaborate. A truly religious man is tolerant, for he loves—Jesus associated with publicans and sinners, and his disciples spoke languages, and went about in the whole world.

My faith: Jesusdom, love of one's neighbour, an effective love, reverence before God. Religiousness is hopeful, it overcomes fear, especially also the fear of death; it urges continually upwards, higher and higher, it feeds the desire for knowledge, and wisdom, it is fearless.

IV

CHRISTIANITY

1. Christianity and the Church

YOU said: Jesusdom. By that are you sug-gesting that the teaching of Jesus did not fully materialize in the Christian churches?

Yes. After all, from its very beginning Christianity does not contain Jesus' teaching alone; it also comprised the Old Testament, and plenty of religious syncretism that was oriental, Greco-Roman, and Hellenistic. It originated among the Jews, but it grew and spread among the Greeks and Romans; it established itself in the educated society of the Roman Empire, among learned theologians like Paul, among philosophers like Augustine and others, but at the same time among uneducated nations and classes, among the barbarians, outcasts, and slaves. Christianity differs according to individuals, classes, nations, and their culture; everybody understands it in his own way. Religion everywhere, and at all times corresponds to the general cultural state of nations, classes and individuals in all its aspects.

One must be cautious in speaking of Christianity as a whole; from the very beginning, and already in Jesus' lifetime there were different conceptions and interpretations of Jesus' teaching, as we see from the New Testament, and these differences became more and more numerous with the spread of Christianity. Remember that of Jesus we do not possess one authentic word, only written and oral tradition has come down from him; there has been preserved an extra-canonical, old Christian literature, fragments of the Gospels, Apocrypha, and such like. In accordance with these different interpretations various church organizations also arose, various doctrines, cults, and so on. The churches, and again from the very beginning, were one against the other; the history of the Christian churches to a large extent is the history of heresy, and of sects as the bigger churches called their schismatic sisters. But this already was taking place with the Jews, Greeks, and Romans, everywhere—just compare, how differently Kant is explained, how many Kantian schools, and tendencies you have. Religion splits up so readily because it offers teaching of the transcendental, inaccessible to experience, and of morality, which varies in accordance with social development, and of subjective religious disposition.

Besides: Every idea deteriorates, and splits up through becoming the property of the masses.

Yes, but the masses, in religion too, have been and still are led by spiritual leaders, as a rule by learned theologians. The first theologian like that was Paul, and the other authors of the New Testament; then the teachers of the Greek Church appeared, who with the help of Greek and Roman philosophy, science, and general culture worked out the first Christian theological systems on the basis of the Old and New Testaments; these especially were the Alexandrian teachers of the end of the Second and the beginning of the Third centuries. The literary fight with the pagans and heretics necessitated that the doctrine should be carefully formulated. Right from its beginning theology was apology and polemic—this is an important point for the understanding of Christianity and of the church; there never was one single and unique Christian church, and Jesus of the New Testament was and still remains mainly the religious leaven.

During the life of Jesus and for quite a long time afterwards the believers and followers only congregated in free corporations—these were the apostolic times; only later was the church systematically organized. With Constantine the church became the state church; the Roman and Byzantine theocracies developed, medieval theocracy followed. The church was no longer merely a religious organization, but also political and secular. The Frankish king Charles the Great with the help of the Pope restored the political Roman imperium; but already in the Eleventh Century conflicts and struggles arose between the emperors and the popes, between the secular and the seculo-spiritual powers, after the Fourteenth Century the papal power noticeably declined; throughout the whole Western Christian world the moral decadence of the church aroused a movement for reform; the church itself set up councils for reform, but without any result; the revolutionary Reformation in Bohemia, then in Germany, and elsewhere came into existence.

It is, sir, a tremendously important historical fact that, and in what way, the church in the Middle Ages took over all spiritual leadership directly, and both directly and indirectly the political one too: the Middle Ages were the time of ecclesiasticizing, modern times become that of de-ecclesiasticizing. In all directions, particularly in philosophy and in the sciences, a new science, with its schools, is arising independent of the church; all ramifications of culture detach themselves from the leadership and control of the church, religion also becomes more individual and independent of the church. The state is secularized, and takes over cultural leadership, of course, more with regard to administration than in actual fact.

Well then this in a nutshell is the development of Christianity as a church; we can see from it how rich and varied are the contents of what we call Christianity.

Christian churches, I have already said, were and still are dependent on their surroundings; they were dependent on their surroundings in ancient times—much more, and deeper than is generally known; Christianity is to a great extent a continuation of antiquity. Just think, the New Testament was written directly in Greek, and the Old Testament by the Third Century before Christ had already been translated into Greek for the Hellenized Jews. It is not easy to say whether Jesus himself became acquainted with Hellenistic ideas; Palestine—especially Jerusalem—and the whole of Asia Minor were already greatly Hellenized in his time. We read in John that the Greeks came to the Apostles and wished to see Christ—they hardly wanted just to see him, they certainly desired to talk with him, possibly then in Greek. Paul must have known Greek, and the Greek philosophy of his time, particularly Stoicism; in John you have a bit of Neoplatonism concerning the logos, and so on. The first Christian theologians were the Greek and Roman philosophers who accepted Christianity; philosophy, chiefly Plato, Aristotle, and the Stoics had an influence on the development of Christian theology, and of ecclesiastical doctrine. The church in the long run took over the whole of Aristotle; altogether the medieval church preserved for us the literature of the antique world together with the languages of Greek and Latin. The state, ruled by the church, took over Roman law and the political ideas of the imperium—take Charles the Great.

The original and the medieval church did not merely take over ancient philosophy, it also took over all sorts of things from ancient religion; there are many institutions in the cult taken over from the religious practices of the Greeks, Romans, and Orientals, particularly the Jews; of course, Christianity changed the sense of the practices and views it adopted——

Well then: did Christianity revolutionize the ancient world, or has it developed out of it?

Both. Every revolution that is not a mere negation and destruction of what is, is a development and a reform. Christianity developed out of Hebrewism, and accepted elements from antiquity; in many points it grew beyond them, in many points it has preserved them. Jesus said himself that he did not come to destroy the law but to fulfil it; de facto, however, he very nearly destroyed it.

The Christian church built up its theology and scholastic philosophy with the help of Greco-Roman philosophy; from the beginning it is apologetical and polemical—by this it proves its dependence on antiquity against which it struggled so long; for every fight is a mutual contact and influence. By its scholastic theology it prepared for the Reformation, the religious and ecclesiastical reform and revolution; by its acceptance of ancient culture it prepared for the Renaissance and Humanism, additional cultural legacies of the ancient world.

According to this the germ of the development of Christianity and of the churches was already contained in the beginnings of Christianity.

Exactly. Take those individual churches, how they are conditioned by historical and evolutionary factors. First of all we have the Catholic Church existing in two formations. As early as the Fifth Century Vincence of Lerino gave rise to the idea of Catholicism as a faith in that quod semper, quod ubique, quod ab omnibus creditum est. The Roman Church represents a spiritual centralization, the perfection and continuation of the political and cultural centralization of the Roman empire; the Eastern church is founded on the federal equality of the autofekal churches and their hierarchs—in the East, on the very fringe of the Orient, Roman centralization no longer had so much power. The difference between ancient Roman culture and the Greco-Oriental one is preserved in the dualism of Rome and Byzantium, of Catholicism and Orthodoxy. One can point to the fact that the Catholic Church in its organization to a large extent took as its model the Roman state; as a social organization it naturally borrowed the patterns of the state organization—because of that it is an organization no less magnificent for the society of that time. Its catholicity and universality is historically unique.

Then we have the Protestant churches. These arose from actual movements to reform the church and morals, but their evolution was already prepared by the gradual detachment of critical reasoning from official theology. Mutatis mutandis, the same thing happens here that once happened in Greece when the philosophers came into conflict with the priestly mythology. Eternal history!

The centralization of Rome finished by developing into the spiritual and religious absolutism of the Roman bishop. Not illogically. If the church is founded by Jesus-God, and if the Roman bishop in apostolic succession is his representative on earth, and the guardian of divine revelation, one may deduce from that the infallibility of the pope. The Eastern church stipulates infallibility for the whole church—in actual fact, for the councils; but a council is a parliament, and has all the defects of parliaments. Similarly the Protestant churches also demand infallibility, but they do not possess that spiritual authority; they give free play to religious and theological subjectivism and individualism, these two fundamental spiritual postulates of modern times. In practice Protestants attribute infallibility to the Scriptures, but the Scriptures are interpreted individually; the Catholic Church therefore watches over the dogmatic interpretation of the Scriptures by its theologians, and controls the translation and reading of the Scriptures by the laymen.

The origin and development of the Reformation, the origin of the new churches and theology is a no less remarkable event in the cultural development of the Christian world; it is wonderful that the Reformation took place, and spread throughout the whole church—the whole development of Christianity is a magnificent and deep drama.

2. *Religious Development with Us*

And our religious development?

I have already spoken about that, and written more than once. When we were first converted to Christianity we wavered between the East and the West; we are geographically on the borders of the East and the West, and Christianity came to us from the East, then still not separated dogmatically from Rome. We soon became religious, political, and cultural Westerners. This attachment to the West is an important and decisive event in our history. Later we, the first in Europe—and again under the influence of the West—carried through the renaissance and revolution of the church: even before our revolution there were individual so-called heretics, and various sects here and there, but with us the Reformation became for the first time an affair of the whole nation. Through the Czech Reformation the ground was prepared for reformation in other countries; Luther was right when he said, we are all Hussites. Hus—Chelcicky—Komensky are our religious leaders, in addition to Western Catholicism. Hus grasped in religion and in the church the pre-eminence of morality; Chelčický noticed the connection between the church and the state, and demanded theocracy; Komenský brought the endeavour of the Reformation to a culmination by his conception that besides religiousness the content of spiritual life is education and humanity, and he imposed on all education the duty that it should be officina humanitatis, the workroom of humanity.

Through the political leadership of the Habsburgs and their Counter-Reformation, forcible in practice, Catholicism again became the church of the majority of the nation, as it was before the revolution of the Reformation. But the violence of the Counter-Reformation was of no advantage to religion; in the Eighteenth Century, during the period of national revival, Enlightenment became the rule, after it, and from it came Liberalism; our aversion to the throne brought with it also dislike of the church, which served that dynasty.

What conclusion can one draw from that for the present time?

What conclusion? Above all things, to know our past—and not to fall into religious indifference. A substantial element of the history of our nation is religious consciousness. The father of the nation, Palacký, was conscious of our special national mission. I have thought a great deal about our religious problem. By nature and fundamentally I am a man of politics, not religious, and not at all theological, but religion is for me the chief component of spiritual life, and of culture as a whole. If in the *Making of a State* I said: Jesus, not Caesar, I said it as a man of politics.

I am, and I used therefore to be an opponent of Liberalism in the form that it took after 1848; for me it is excessively rationalistic, and in religious questions too indifferent, too sterile.

Can the churches still develop? Is there the possibility of some religious revival?

Everything develops; there is and there will be religious development too. I tried to gain an understanding of the leading Christian churches; I lived Catholicism deeply and personally, later I learned to know Protestantism, and penetrated as far as I was able into Orthodoxy, especially of the Russian type; I am aware of the spiritual state of all these leading churches, and I do not know why it should be final. Everywhere now we see mankind, nations move towards unity in all spheres of activity—please don't let us be confused because that takes place with so much difficulty; big things do not appear in a moment. In the Christian churches also there is a desire for one fold, and one shepherd. Well, yes, attempts are being made to unite the churches; they have been repeating themselves for centuries among the Catholic churches, as well as among the

Protestant ones. Catholicism refuses to unite with the Protestants, but prominent leaders on both sides show unprecedented signs of a conciliatory spirit. Even slow history is history. Of course: to unite the churches without reviving religiousness and morality—that would not be any solution of the present internal religious problem. Religion is a whole, it cannot be patched up.

If I believe in the teaching of Jesus, I believe, I must also believe, in the future of religion. In any case then, and particularly here do I refer to Palacký, in our circumstances we must ask for toleration—not toleration arising from religious indifference but a positive toleration: everybody to hold his own, to have his conviction, but to respect the true convictions of others. Grudge truth to no man—that was said to us, and it is valid for ever.

Notice how greatly religious sects have increased with us along with political freedom, a Czechoslovak church with considerable membership has also arisen; no doubt, many look upon that as a crumbling of religion—but at any rate it is not religious indifference. Our republic is not only varied with respect to nationalities but also with respect to religion; I see in that the possibility of religious development and of spiritual development as a whole.

3. Church and State

You said that you are more a man of politics than a man of religion. Surely then you look upon the church sub specie of politics.

That is understood. Every organization, especially one so huge as a church, is ipso facto a political reality. In a pagan state the church developed against it, and partly also with it; as an organized society it 'must of necessity determine its relation to the state, which at that time was the only universal social organization. Jesus himself adjudged to Caesar what was Caesar's, and Paul went even farther in that direction. The church did not attempt to abolish the pagan state, or to reform it politically, but to convert it to Christianity; when it had become Christianized, and made the church a state affair, Christian theocracy appeared. In the church the state found its moral and religious foundations; the monarchs—nota bene the absolute monarchs—were "by divine grace." In the East, theocracy took on the character of Caesaro-Papism, in the West, the papacy rose above Caesar and Caesarism, thus Papo-Caesarism. It was natural and right at the time that the church as the vehicle of culture should assume primacy over the state, but this primacy did not last long, and the struggle began between the spiritual and secular powers.

The relation between church and state gradually became stable. Remember that for a considerable time, when the Christians were becoming numerous, and the church was becoming· centralized, the Roman emperors persecuted the Christians; true, historians now point out that there was not so much persecution as used to be said before, but that does not alter the matter at all. If the heathen persecuted the Christians, the latter did so to the heathen, when and wherever they came into power—Jesus, I have said, was a leaven, and his prescription of love was not given effect immediately and everywhere. One can find many humanitarian mottoes from the earliest Christian imes; I refer only to Tertullian: "The divine standard and the human standard do not go together, Christ's flag and the devil's. A Christian can only fight without the sword—the Lord did away with the sword."

The dependence of the church on the state; you can see it most clearly in the way in which the division of the Roman empire into an Eastern and a Western one prepared the ground for the origin and the development of the Roman, and the Greek Orthodox Catholicism. There were, of course, cultural differences as well, but the influence of the state on the church is clearly evident here.

The church in itself by its substance is a social institution; besides doctrine and ritual it is the guardian and initiator of morality, and of the whole conduct of life. From this point the springing up of theocracies of various types: religion and politics, church and state lead society jointly by the hand——usually so that the church leads the king, and the princes. Through the Reformation the relation of the church to the state was altered; the state acquired greater power in that as regards the Catholics it protected the church against the Reformation, and itself carried through the Counter-Reformation; as regards the Protestants it was the patron and the direct master of the new churches which in the meantime were occupied with the elaboration of their theology, and ecclesiastical organization. Protestantism was more democratic, Catholicism more aristocratic.

Well, true; orthodox political science and jurisprudence do not see in theocracy the foundations of the state and of the law; brought up as they are on Roman law, lawyers explain the substance and the development of the law and of the state as being independent of religion, ethics, and morality. For them besides ethics and morality law is an independent and original sociological

118

category. Well, I can't help it; I imagine law and the state as being built upon moral foundations, and in that respect also on religious ones. It is admissible, and development tends in that direction, that the spiritual and the secular powers should be separate in politics, and in administration; the state originated in the need for social organization, to a large extent its origin was military and economic; but it also administered justice, protected those who suffered injury, punished the culprits—to the extent that the state calls itself a legal and cultural state, it places itself on a moral foundation. Of course, through the development and increasing complexity of social relations, the economic, administrative, and military functions gain the upper hand. But even in the old theocracies a truncheon, should I say, was stronger than arguments, spiritual power was and is more permanent, but secular power is stronger. But one must realize that human society is directed by two main organizations, by the state and the church, and that these organizations naturally and necessarily are continually adjusting their mutual relations; the thrones supported the altar, the altar supported the thrones.

Only in modern times has a third element been added to the state and religion—the national idea; but that already is another chapter.

V

THE SO-CALLED CULTURAL CONFLICT

1. *Faith and Science*

THE situation with regard to religion and culture today is seen objectively in our universities: in addition to the three, four, secular faculties, scientific and philosophical, we have the theological faculty; ex officio two world views are being offered which differ in their methods, teaching, and aim. In opposition to one another, on the one side stands science with scientific philosophy, for which experience and reason are the sources of all knowledge; and on the other ecclesiastical theology, which proclaims revelation and ecclesiastical authority as the fount of true knowledge. The same state supports and pays for the institutions and for their exponents; both not only criticize each other, but reject and exclude. Here in a nutshell you have the cultural conflict, even if such conflicts do not always take place directly and openly.

Today that fight has almost been brought to a

conclusion, hasn't it? At least it appears that men have other worries.

Brought to a conclusion, that is, to an end, it is not. It is true that at times it is more radical and pronounced, at other times quieter and indirect, but it is a chronic antagonism. Apparently it is the leaven of cultural development. People are not sufficiently aware that that spiritual antagonism has persisted in Europe much longer than two thousand years. Its beginnings were with the Greeks. As soon as science and philosophy had become detached from traditional mythology and polytheism the antagonism arose: Socrates—a typical and beautiful example of a thinker, and one of the first victims of that cultural conflict. After Socrates, in an ethical and religious sense, philosophy always runs counter to popular religion. Christianity continues the fight against polytheism and mythology, and stabilizes its theology by means of Greek philosophy, even if, at the same time, it fights that philosophy apologetically; but simultaneously it also takes over from the Greek and Oriental world many mythological, religious, and ritualistic elements—in other words, it assimilates the whole of that classic conflict. From that time onwards the conflict has continued.

I should say, with the exception of the Middle Ages.

Not quite. In the Middle Ages there was an urge for unity, but it was not completely realized. We always have apologetics and disputes even if weaker than in the original church; there were less disputes with Islam than with ancient philosophy, for the very reason that those disputes were being settled by resort to arms. The church organized its philosophy—scholastics—as "the handmaid of theology"; but this very subjection points to the inner antagonism—like every subjection. Scholasticism by its reasoning, more shrewd than objective, by its defence of theology, de facto, undermined the authority of the church; after all, isn't it a contradiction in adiecto when the divine word, the word revealed by God, has to be defended by human reason, and when that reason, criticism, and speculation must decide upon the value of various revelations and of religious doctrines. Reason must decide the value of the teaching of Moses, Jesus, Mohammed. Already in the Eleventh Century the Schoolmen helped themselves out with the teaching of a double truth—here indeed you have palpable antagonism. And take that continual appearance of heretics, and sects, and arguments against them—arguments supported by fire and sword; a continual cultural fight. The definition of Vincence of Lerino is valid, and always was valid only for conceptual and ideal catholicity.

The medieval church made certain of the course to its authority, it dictated the uniform view of the world by its spiritual and political absolutism; but this absolutism did not maintain itself for long, it could not—it bore within itself the intellectual and secular legacy from the ancient world. Scholasticism by its continual apologetics, by its logic and appeal to reason, by its acceptance of ancient philosophy, mainly that of Aristotle, the supreme Greek rationalist, prepared the way for the Reformation, Humanism, and the Renaissance. And so modern times arise, consciously overcoming times that are past—modern times against the Middle Ages; modern science arises, and modern philosophy based on science. Art also ceases to serve nothing but the church —the Renaissance by its very name indicates the contrast between the Middle Ages and modern times.

Also the state, and the whole social organization, detaches itself from the church. Catholic theology finds itself in conflict on the one hand with the new Protestant theologies, on the other with science and the new philosophy—and last but not least, with the new conception of the state as well. The new theological Protestant systems were nearer to the new philosophy and politics than Catholicism; Protestantism accepted the principle of religious individualism, abolished the priesthood, and by that step in principle weakened ecclesiasticism, the theocratic hierachy. Of course, Protestantism also stood for ecclesiastical and theological absolutism—Calvin had Servetus burned.

On the whole: the Middle Ages were rather disjoined in their substance; the ecclesiastical and political unity, and the uniform view of the world were artificial, they were achieved by authority, by physical and spiritual violence. And therefore modern times arose, the conscious ecclesiastical revolution, and then also the political one against the medieval social organization.

The present times are characterized by secularization; against the church the state is ever gaining greater and wider power, the secularization of all social functions and powers is taking place; in place of ecclesiastical absolutism the absolutism of the state is arising. Protestantism, especially of the Lutheran type, to a certain extent also supported this absolutism; in the struggle against Catholicism and the papacy, the state acquired strength. It is no accident that a prominent modern Protestant theologian came to the conclusion that the church could cease to exist, and hand over all control of society to the state. Catholicism also at that time assisted the state in carrying through the Counter-Reformation with the help of the state power——here and there the state came to the support of the churches for its own benefit.

Well, this conflict of rational philosophy and science with theology, this conflict and struggle of critical reason with the ecclesiastical and religious authority is chronic, it arises from the very nature and development of human thought. Science and philosophy already with the Greeks, and to the present day, have developed from original myth; the human spirit matures by getting rid of mythology——true, that movement away from mythology, that scientific process of becoming more exact, has taken place, and continually does take place by gradual stages; a bit of science found its way into the myth, at times a bit of myth has adhered to the science. Of course, mankind could not wait until science and philosophy could provide it with a complete, logically and homogeneously constructed, scientifically exact view of the world and of life; people were in need of an explanation of the world and of life straight away, take it where you can; and that original explanation was and again continues to be mythical. And, of course, when that conflict flares up acutely, criticism is often replaced from this and that side by hostile agitation: the church wants to suppress science, science wants to refuse religion. But negation is not and cannot be the aim, positive development, progress, and perfection in this and that direction are the things that matter.

But can faith be perfected through knowledge?

Mind the word—faith! Psychologically faith is judgement and the conviction that that judgement is right; in that sense faith is a fundamental activity of reason, and there is no knowledge without faith. Epistemologically the point is whether our believing is scientific, critical, or if instead of correct observation, and giving the facts, we believe in what we desire; the question is whether we accept authority—or critical reason. Science also believes, but with giving the facts.

That is positive progress: For instance, Greek philosophy opposed itself to popular mythology and religious polytheism; it was working its way away from myth to the beginnings of science, and in religion to monotheism. Because of that this philosophy was agreeable to Jewish and Christian monotheism and it helped to stabilize Christian theology. The Greek philosophers also had come to proclaim the humanity and the equality of all men; in this Christianity continued by preaching love and human kindness. Here you have such an example of positive development: Christian theology took over the philosophy of the ancient world although ex thesi it stood against it. And similarly later: theology elaborated its Christian philosophy and this, perforce, opened the way to modern scientific philosophy. And present-day science—we are only on the threshold of knowledge, but how much deeper can our understanding be of the order of the world, and of life with each new scientific advance! The more we widen and deepen our picture of the world, and of life, by scientific knowledge, the better we know, or are in a position to know God the creator, and mover.

I express it like this: philosophy is the organ of science, of the scientific, critical spirit, theology is the organ of myth and of the mythical spirit; the mythical spirit is not dead, and possibly cannot die. The scientists and philosophers in the heat of the struggle against theology easily fail to see that theology is not religion. What does it mean if in spite of that eternal struggle of theology with science and philosophy, religion and the churches still persist? Religion is not merely a theoretical question, what matters in it is not only the view of life and ot the world, theology is not the only point, but it is a question of life itself, it is a practical affair. To the extent that the churches fulfil the religious needs of living people, they live themselves. It would do philosophers no harm if they realized that lots and lots of metaphysical systems about which they teach with serious faces from the objective and scientific standpoint are no better, no less mythological than theology. And among the philosophical systems also, isn't there a perpetual conflict and struggle?

There is of course a difference here: philosophy tries to convince man but it does not desire to exercise authority over souls.

It doesn't do that? It does, but only by other means; isn't the teaching of scientific knowledge also the directing of souls? Haven't we also got scientific churches, sects, and heretics? A scientist, a philosopher communicates his thoughts, and findings to people just in the same way as the priests and preachers set forth their doctrine. All thinking and doing is not only individual, it is also social; we don't think for ourselves alone, but for others, and with them. Sir, if philosophy could it would have wished many times to command. The scientists and philosophers will at times also claim the sole disposal of the means of grace and infallibility as certain as not. Think of it, the scientists and philosophers also are only men, and for man it is not always a matter of truth, but also of glory, prestige, bread, and such like.

That means: in the cultural fight not to drive out the Devil with Beelzebub.

And not to pour the baby out with the bath-water. Time and again in the struggle against religion and theology one forgets that religion is not merely doctrine, merely theology, that it is the content of life, that it permeates, and uplifts the whole life of those who believe.

Let us say: in its cult and ceremony the church has, should I call it, its poetry. I remember— just imagine how Bjornson described the influence of the church on the village—just imagine it in all its fullness; how that unusual, architectonically and symbolically inspiring building itself affects a simple man, and especially a child which knows only a poor, cramped room; the villagers see themselves in the church all together, all washed, all dressed up, from the mayor—at one time from the feudal lord—down to the last cottager, and they all belong to one body; here the young people meet, the lovers in their best attire—that also, sir, is part of the thing; in church people listen to music, often good music, and they sing with the unity of minds; the statues, pictures, and incense, all that affects them almost sensually;

129

the ritual, and the individual ceremonies, it is like a theatre, it is a drama, and at the same time a great symbol, a spectacle, and stimulus to thought; the sermon is an example of rhetoric, discussion, and argument, an example in how to develop some given theme—how many pleasant impressions there are, what a feast for the senses, and for the souls of man, what it means for the children! What it meant at one time for me! That's it, it is not enough to deny theology in theory: religion and morality are lived in practice; one may give people another doctrine, but what is one to give for that religious expectancy and fullness? Only a living religion can take the place of a religion and ecclesiasticism that is moribund and vegetating. In this the philosophers and theologians make their mistake: theology is not religion, it is only the theory of religion; philosophy can take the place of theology, but it cannot take the place of religion. Of course— the churches also often attach greater importance to theology than to what men believe, to orthodoxy than to the moral and living content of religion. But isn't that the same, for instance, in the political parties? A human weakness: we attach more importance to words, than to deeds. . . .

2. *Tolerance*

In that historical conflict between science and the churches I see one only way: not to lose religiousness in the continual search for knowledge. A decent, honest man will be tolerant—will also be critical of himself, and of his views. I remember Augustine: in necessariis unitas, in dubiis libertas, in omnibus caritas—true, this Augustine also approved of capital punishment for heretics.

And yet, as you know, believers and unbelievers look upon tolerance with distrust: because thou art lukewarm, and neither cold nor hot, I will spue thee out of my mouth.

Yes; but tolerance is not lukewarm nor comfortable, it is not wavering and vague; in tolerance, too, there must be courage and consistency. Tolerance is not indifference, it is not a moral and religious flabbiness, and lack of conviction. I have always blamed modern Liberalism for its indifference to questions of religion and morals. Where there is lively interest and participation there can be no place for indifference. I do not admit "laisser faire"—that is not co-operation. Liberalism as is now understood is usually only a political and economical programme, but that is not enough. Liberalism had its origin as "free

131

thought" in the first place against creeds' and churches, in the second against political servitude. But liberty is not an empty frame into which anybody may put what he likes; real freedom makes space for better understanding, better organization, and more reasonable action. Tolerance is a modern virtue, it is true humanity; we are aware that we are differently and variously endowed by nature; therefore we hasten towards spiritual and social unity, not as a result of authority, and violence but by recognizing the various gifts of human nature, and their harmonization. Unity today and in the future we can only achieve through harmony, collaboration, and therefore through tolerance. I have got here a nice quotation from Goethe:

"Die verschiedenen Denkweisen sind in der Verschiedenheit der Menschen gegründet, und eben deshalb ist eine durchgehende gleichförmige Überzeugung unmöglich. Wenn man nun weiss, auf welcher Seite man steht, so hat man schon genug getan; man ist alsdann ruhig gegen sich und billig gegen andre." (Goethe and Reinhard.)

Frequently the theologians—in the interest of religion, they say—complain of reason and modern scepticism. Unjustly. Surely theology itself only exists for the purpose of demonstrating religious doctrine to reason; and what finally decides the value of those different churches and dogmas in their perpetual strife? Again only reason. And with regard to scepsis—scepsis is not irreligion; the real enemy of religion, the genuine atheism and fall from God is indifference, indifferentism, and cynicism. Indifferentism and cynicism are the mortal disease of religion, and of spiritual life altogether, they are spiritual death. Many a sceptic, and even an atheist, has more religion than a vapid religious churchgoer. All his life Jesus denounced the mere conventional church-goers; to the gentlemen of the temple of Jerusalem he seemed to be a godless man.

Well yes, at times men sicken of this conflict, and their hearts draw them both to the science and the faith, they have no desire to lose this or that; well, they seek a compromise, concessions are made. . . . I have watched these attempts, but I cannot see in them the true way. In the very latest philosophy a certain degree of irra-tionalism is appearing, the will, or feelings, or instincts are left to decide. One can hear the cry for myth as if myth were religion. That is a great mistake; neither myth, nor theology, nor science, nor philosophy is religion. Religion can be conceived mythologically and theologically, it can be conceived scientifically, and philosophi-cally; but such things are only theories of religion,

133

while religion—is just religion, life in God and with God.

And to cry for myth—as if in these days there were not enough myths and mythologians! Kant with his a priorism finds himself in myth, and in the end concedes a "more subtle" anthropomorphism, Schelling, Fichte, Hegel are mythmakers, Nietzsche creates a myth of the superman, Comte becomes a philosophical fetishist, Darwin, Heckel, and the Monists are sunk in myth up to their ears—we have no cause to return to myth, the task is always: to think critically—and to live religiously.

3. State and Church

It seems to me that if the churches were ONLY in conflict with philosophy and science the conflict would be more or less ex cathedra. . . . I mean to say, not so historical and collective, as it really is. After all, this is a question of the ecclesiastical, secular, and social order.

You are right. Historically like this: The church arose in the Roman state; in the Ancient World the state was the only universal social organization, and that is why it had so much power. Remember that the Roman emperors—like the oriental despots, and possibly also under the influence of the Orient—were deified; the Roman principate and Caesarism were already pure theocracy. Augustus carried out religious reforms, and the persecution of the Christians originated in leanings towards theocracy. The medieval church won its victory over the empire in matters of philosophy and organization, a more perfect theocracy arose, that is, a more religious one. The development of modern times from the Reformation and the Renaissance, the development of culture and society, I have already described as a gradual secularization; hand in hand with it went cultural differentiation. The medieval church covered and directed religion, belief, knowledge, and thought; it forced art to be subservient; for its own ends it monopolized charity, social welfare, hospitals, and all education; it gave consent to marriage; it intervened in international affairs, and looked after the development of the colonies. In it the spirit of universalism and cosmopolitanism of the Roman empire still persisted. And now think how one thing after another breaks away from the ancient ecclesiastical system: new churches split off, and begin careers of their own; science, philosophy, art became independent of the church; the states, in medieval theocracy subservient to the church, take over the leadership of society in all directions; the state takes charge of school management, education, social welfare, social legislation; all that is a genuine, even if silent, separation of the state from the church, which did not wait for formal partition. Medieval Catholicism with its universalism and internationalism was valuable and essential; in the Barbarian flood it saved the Greek and Roman civilization—it was not in vain that the church preserved the language of the Roman empire—and laid the foundations for the whole of that European civilization, fundamentally international, supernational, cosmopolitan. Notice that the cultures of the Orient remained chiefly national. The church gave to the races and nations of Europe that cosmopolitanism, that message to go out into all the world, and teach all nations. That age-long process of secularization, of de-ecclesiasticization is, and will continue to be, historically necessary, it cannot be reversed nor stopped. In it the church and religion must find their proper place and bring to consciousness their new task.

I have already said that the power of the state did not arise through secularization alone but also through alliance with the churches; secularization is a long, persistent, and still incomplete process. The Catholic dynasties carried through the Counter-Reformation—in that lay the foundation of secular absolutism. But against that political revolutions broke out and still break out, as the revolution of the Reformation broke out against the ecclesiastical absolutism; from the ecclesiastical crisis developed a political crisis of the state, and this also is still going on. The churches do not understand clearly enough this cultural process and they cannot reconcile themselves with it, they strive to regain the power they have lost. If they adapted themselves to the changed conditions, they would find for themselves a new and a higher function: a purely spiritual function, and truly religious. The more order in the world is secularized, the more the churches could and should dedicate themselves to a pure and immaculate religion — to Jesus' religion: to make the world truly Christian, not through power but through love.

A cultural process. . . . After all, such a collective, eternal process is taking place in people's souls. My whole life long I have seen how the conflict between theology and philosophy, between spiritual and secular order, according to fate, manifests itself in the mental disorders, upsets, and half-heartedness of our times and of living people. That problem I already put before myself in *Suicide*—but I refer to it again and again, the last time in *The Making of a State*. . . . I always thought, and wrote not as a result of my own philosophical system, but because that crisis of the age drove me to it—you will understand, sir, that I lived it in myself . . . for myself and for others.

You speak of the crisis of the churches; isn't there also today a crisis in religion?

Not to the same extent; paying no attention to the fact that the crisis is not an end, and doom, but just a crisis. Certainly it is not the end of religion. What many people take to be a definite movement away from religion is sometimes a desire for another religion, one that is living, pure, and more perfect. But it is true that there also arises the scientific ochlocracy of highbrow mandarins, I should say of the snobs of science and of semi-science; and every ochlocracy, sir, is only for a time.

You see that now philosophers and scientists take risks for religion, possibly more effectively than theologians. Nothing strange; scientists and philosophers must be aware that they cannot replace religion.

A religious crisis: in fact, the crisis of the Christian churches. The chief problem in dispute between theology and science is revelation, whether, in fact, religion is based on revelation, or whether some natural religion is possible. Putting it quite frankly, the deity of Jesus is the

138

problem. Orthodoxy asserts that Christianity was founded by Jesus-God, that his teaching is divine revelation, that the church is a divine institution; from this further consequences follow with regard to doctrine and practice. Natural religion, on the contrary, asserts that Jesus was a man like any other, and in this very fact it sees the higher sanction of Christianity, namely that a man alone without any miracle, through his own personality raised himself so high. In this way religion becomes a natural gift of man, like science, art, and suchlike, and by our own efforts it can be perfected in us like the other gifts of human nature. Our life acquires a special value if a man of his own self can be as perfect as Jesus demanded, and achieved as a man. I repeat, I am not a theologian, I am not a teacher of religion, I am merely a man of religious faith; to follow Jesus, that is enough for me.

Are you for the religious education of children?

Of course, I am; surely that follows from the value of religion. But for religious education the teaching of the catechism in schools is not enough. A school today is scientific, that is, it is founded on scientific concepts; if in it the usual catechism is taught inevitably a theological and religious crisis already breaks out in childhood and adolescence. It is not even necessary to mention that

the TEACHING of religion is not religious EDUCA-
TION. The fight for the school is a difficult problem
in our transient age.

*An indiscreet question: are you pleading for religion
only as a philosopher—or also as a politician?*

As an answer I shall give you one experience:
when the priests in the churches began to pray
for the Republic, and the President, Švehla called
attention to its great political significance. He
was right. We should be able to appreciate it
when an organization so big and old becomes
reconciled with our secular and democratic order.
By it my relation to religion was not changed. I
have been defending religion since time out of
mind, I have had it since childhood, it did not
forsake me even at the time when I was defamed
as an atheist. . . . My philosophy of religion I
have already told you. And I have also told you
that by nature I am a man of politics: problems
of religion must be solved in practice by those
people who by their talents are religious, the
geniuses and leaders of religion. We live in a
time of transition: teachers of faith, hope and
charity are wanting with us. But as a theist I
believe in the future of religion.

VI

STILL ON RELIGION

1. *Religious Life*

I AM returning again to religion: surely the feeling of religiousness is not enough for a religious life; every religion must rest upon some positive doctrine.

Look here—religion doesn't let even you alone!

I understand that my philosophy of religion as I first outlined it does not satisfy you, and it does not satisfy your critical reason. I shall try to formulate the main points again, and you must not be impatient if I repeat myself here and there.

Yes, every religion must be formulated, it has then its doctrine, its creed, dogma, and theology; but every religion must also be practised and lived. I do not hesitate to say: lived intensely. For me, the leader and teacher of religion is Jesus. Jesus was not a theologian, he was a prophet, the greatest of the prophets: what genius is for art, science, politics, and other spheres, the prophet is for religion. A prophet—that doesn't merely mean to prophesy, and foresee, but to proclaim the divine word, to rebuke, and to lead, to lift up to a new and more spiritual life; to be an example, to be the voice of conscience, to be the awakener of life—it is not easy to express it in a word.

According to the teaching of Jesus religion is faith in the only God, Creator, Director of the world, Father; but Jesus does not overstrain transcendentalism, his religion is not solely for heaven, it is for the earth, and for daily, ordinary life. He did not speak much of the beginnings, or of the end of the world, he did not occupy himself with history, like the Old Testament, which in that also was only a national religion and doctrine. Jesus' religion reveals itself in morality and humanity, it is humanitarianism sub specie aeternitatis. The difference between religiousness and morality we express with the words: holy and good. Holiness is moral life in God.

Can morality exist without religion?

It can; sometimes it is better than the morality of the religious and church-going people—the question simply is, what that religiousness is like, and what that morality is like. To go to church, to pray, to perform ceremonies, out of habit, and so on, that is easy; but to be fully and constantly aware of one's relation to God, to respect every man, and to help him, to suppress one's egoism, to live reasonably and morally—that is different, and that is true religiousness. Morality and spiritual life can exist without religion and outside of religion, but tell me: are they complete and perfect? According to my reasoning, no. I postulate religion as a necessary consummation of spiritual and cultural life; by seeing in morality the chief component of religion, I make out of morality a religious cult. To live morally is the real worship of God.

Are faith in God and morality sufficient for a full religious life?

They are not. Even in the New Testament we read that devils also believe in God, but tremble. If we want to use the word FAITH, then religious faith must be a personal relation, and an intimate relation with God. Faith can be a mere hypothesis; except that we do not push through to God merely by speculation. When transcendentalism is over-emphasized in religion one easily forgets one's neighbour and the moral life; subordinate religious elements, church-going and ritual are too greatly accentuated and over-valued; also one falls into a lifeless, anti-living, too life-denying exaltation as you see in ascetics, anchorites, people who mutilate the body and the spirit. Tell me, weren't those people acknowledged as saints who lived on pillars, and believed that in that way they were serving God; others again let themselves be eaten alive by vermin, and I don't know what else. In that itself lies the over-emphasis on the transcendent; people. want to serve God with something special and unnatural—religious acrobatics! Yes, I also reject religious mysticism; to merge into one with God by suppressing reason and physical life, to concentrate so much that one falls into a trance, and intoxication, and in such a state to cohabit with the deity—all that is more or less pathological. Religion is not a matter of nerves and paroxysms, but the bringing into consciousness of the sense of life into the consciousness of a normal man, healthy in body and spirit. But there is also religious pathology, there are delirious aberrations, and pure mental illness, there is also religious ignorance—"God's people" of a Russian mushik are a strange race—I have seen them and observed them! You know that people also used to worship epilepsy and madness as a divine manifestation. In that also there is an over-emphasis of the transcendent, or more concretely: the need of mystery and mysteriousness.

Can religion exist entirely without mystery?

It cannot; but it depends upon what mysteries we acknowledge. In actual fact the world and life are mysterious to us—how much do we really know and comprehend? Man has a natural feeling for the mysterious: the world is a mystery to man, and man is a mystery to himself—isn't that

unobserved flower in the field a mystery? Just
have a good look at it—from where does its
beauty, its fitness, from where does it all come?

In his weakness, misery, and distress man longs
for miracles and revelations—in everything and
everywhere; in pleasure and in sickness, in politics and in social yearnings, in the metaphysical
problems of the soul and of life. From that comes
that delight in occultism, and in so-called mysterious phenomena.

My God, mysterious phenomena! As if the
fact that I perceive this whole world, that I see
that tree there, that I admire it, that I am conscious of the mystery of its life and growth—as
if in all that there were not phenomena just as
wonderful, just as mysterious! After all, is the
soul after death something more mysterious and
recondite than the soul while one is alive, and the
soul of those we call great something more
wonderful than the soul of that woman there who
is raking hay?

When they are immersed in their nearest surroundings people cannot see the greatness in all
things; every inconspicuous thing, and the most
trivial event, is something mysterious and tremendous! Let us not be deluded by habit—we have
above all things got used to ourselves, we have
become accustomed to see only as far as our

nearest surroundings, but just let us think, just let us have a good look at these familiar persons and things, and we shall widen our views of the mysterious and the miraculous!

2. On Religiousness

What is religiousness in a psychological sense? A relation to God, a personal relation, can be experienced in various ways; to some extent every man feels it in a different way; in this as well, through our personalities, every one of us is individual, with different endowments, and special experiences. For the Old Testament the beginning of wisdom and of true religiousness was the fear of the Lord; to the present day the words God-fearing and religious are linked together; also with the Greeks and the Romans the relation of the man to the gods and the deity was δεισι-δαιμονία, θεοσέβεια. In Aristotle I found the literal statement that man cannot love God. Jesus described the relation of man to God as love and filial relation; God is a father to man, we are sons to Him. That is a new definition of religiousness and of religion, and by means of this Christianity rose above the ancient world. In the Old Testament, it is true, there is something of a family relation to God, in so far as Jehovah was the God of the family, tribe, or nation.

Jesus linked together love of God with love of one's neighbour, and this divine sonship and the mutual love of the sons of heaven he made universal; love of one's neighbour is valid for all men and all nations. By it faith in the one God reaches its culmination: there is only one God, God of all nations and of all men.

Jesus accepted the Old Testament, he did not come, as he said, to destroy but to fulfil. Jesus did not create religion, that always existed, and for a long time before him; he was a reformer. The Christian churches took over the Old Testament as well, and in addition to the love of Jesus they kept alive the Old Testament timor Domini —more than was necessary.

Besides this relation towards God and towards one's neighbour, there are still further elements in religion that we can distinguish; ritual, ceremonies, religious institutions evoke stronger feelings in the faithful, often stronger than is the feeling for the invisible God. The relation towards the hierarchy, the priests, and preachers, dependence on the church and on its leaders is —in the same way as in politics and in other spheres—an important element in religion. Since there are so many elements, and since everyone can select something else, sometimes even quite an outward and minor thing, some ceremony, perhaps, or some article of faith, there is not one single kind of religiousness: God is one only, but the personal relation towards Him differs at different times and with different men.

Religious life—like all other activities—easily becomes mechanical; so, for instance, going to church on Sundays, or every day, making the sign of the cross, praying, and so on, can become a purely mechanical habit; with many people religion is nothing more than a habit—you know, don't you, those so-called devout women praying with their lips.

Praying—yes.

I can see in my mind's eye the statue of an American sculptor, an Indian on his horse: the horse stands as if it could understand its rider who is lifting his mind to the Great Spirit, with his arms outstretched, his eyes raised to the sky —a true, beautiful prayer.

Of course, we cannot express our religious relation to God in any other way than by the concepts of our empirical psychology. The theologians themselves say that God to us is an inaccessible being.

Just because of God's inaccessibility a strong element of religiousness in all religions is respect

to the founders of religions and of the churches:
to Buddha, Moses, Mohammed, and of course
also to Jesus. The Christian mystics and the
ordinary religious believers too, direct their love
more towards Jesus than towards God; Christian
theology as a whole identifies God with Jesus.
Apotheosis, deification in all religions is nothing
more than an attempt to bring nearer to oneself,
in some way to humanize the inaccessible deity
incomprehensible to sense and to reason. And so
art, architecture, sculpture and painting, poetry,
music, the song and the dance often express
religious ideas more effectively than theological
terms. This Moses, however much out of fear
of idolatry he prohibited material representations
of God, strove to depict Him in words, definitions, and by way of the whole history of divine
revelation — pure anthropomorphism. That is
human and natural; we necessarily portray the
inaccessible deity in a human way, we cannot do
it otherwise; but at least we must try to conceive
it spiritually. The brother of Jesus, James, when
describing pure and immaculate religion could
not say more than that we ought to visit the
orphans and widows in their affliction, and maintain ourselves untouched by worldliness; and
John in his Epistle writes the phrase that we
have already quoted that a man cannot love

the invisible God without loving his visible neighbour.

By thinking scientifically a man overcomes mystical anthropomorphism, he overcomes it through his reason and feelings; taught by Jesus he overcomes the religion of fear and dread and replaces it with respect towards God and love towards his neighbour.

I should denote my relation to God by the Latin reverentia—reverence full of trust and hopefulness. And as for the love of one's neighbour, I accept that commandment in its full meaning, as recommended by Jesus: that we should also love an enemy—it is possible, even if it is difficult. That does not deprive me of the right and duty to resist wrongdoing and oppression; but I try to be honourable and just to my enemy. There was a fine element in the old chivalry, which during the combat, and after the combat imposed respect towards opponents. When Jesus drove the money-changers out of the temple he did not conceal his indignation; indignation is not hatred.

Religion, that is not only the relation of man to God but also the relation of man to man. I say to myself: can pure, complete love of one's neighbour exist without the highest appreciation of the human personality, without faith in the immor-

tality of the human soul? I know all the objections
of the materialists, pantheists, enlightened men,
and so on; but love of one's neighbour, natural
love, and needing no proofs—is it not itself a
proof of what man ought to and must be to us?
I refer to Jesus in love of one's neighbour, I refer
to Plato in acknowledgement of immortality. In
that respect I am a Platonist—I side with Plato
also against those modern theologians who are
somewhat at a loss with faith in immortality;
they stick it into apologetics and other doctrines,
and leave it out of dogma. I am the more pleased
with Plato because he pointed out the importance
of that teaching also by way of method.

Religiousness is a special state of truthfulness:
to a religious man life and the world are like a
classic drama, but without the satirical ending;
classical drama by its very origin and substance
was a religious manifestation. Life is not a farce,
or a comedy, or a tragedy, it is a drama; it is
never without greatness, without the logic of fate
—to have a bit of humour in it does not do any
harm: Shakespeare understood this very well.
Surely, Jesus also smiled, for in love there is joy.
Through religion we grasp the importance of life,
its seriousness and value—and its beauty. Divine
majesty and greatness fill us with reverence and
devotion. Religion also gives part of that great-

ness to us—only a small part, which does not deprive us of natural humility; real religion overcomes titanism. Remember how the Old Testament begins with titanism; the serpent promises the first parents that they will be like gods—Goethe's *Faust* in his titanism really begins with Adam. Why not, the titan! Doesn't he say himself: mir fehlt der Glaube.

Religiousness is individual, but it does not admit solipsism; in religiousness itself there is the acknowledgement of the world external to us, of the world of God, and of the world of one's neighbour.

Religion overcomes loneliness in us; just imagine clearly what it means to be alone! I have often observed myself in absolute solitude; with us Nature is too rich for us to have the full sensation; in the desert that sensation is richer. Jesus also used to go into the desert—meditation requires solitude. Concentration is necessary for man but it cannot be a vocation; therefore hermits did not live normal lives. Life requires work for oneself and for one's neighbours; we must not run away from the difficulties of life and the world, we must overcome the world. The life of the monk and of the hermit as a state and an occupation is in fact the mechanization of solitude; not concentration, but habit—or profession.

I know, metaphysical inquisitiveness can and does enquire for still more things; but you wanted to hear my credo; its last word is reverentia: a conscious reverence before God and before man; in this reverence for one's neighbour, love, I say also, conscious love, is included.

3. Faith and Reason

You lay stress on consciousness, and so on reason, also in religion.

Yes, as in everything; everywhere we must lay stress on critical, comparative reason. Religiousness is a natural state of man. Even Paul acknowledged natural religion alongside of the revealed, or supernatural one; and also today one says: anima naturaliter christiana. This natural religion, it is just that through our own reason, and abilities we become conscious of the world and of our relation to it. Faith in the deity, our relation to God, in short, religion is a result of deep thought, and of the experience of the ages; each one of us consciously or unconsciously links up with this historical development and tradition of a thousand years. A thinking man simply desires and must make clear for himself: what the world is, who made it, what is God, what we ourselves are, what we are aiming for, what death is; in the very end all these questions concentrate into one: What, who am I really? Well, yes, these questions and their answers strongly excite our feelings, rouse our hopes, and move our will; therefore we overlook in them the intellectual element— but we have already spoken about that. So-called emotional knowledge, intuition, enlightenment, inspiration, vision, and so on, all those are momentary, sensual, and intellectual observations, or judgements which we attribute to the accompanying emotional and mental excitement. That is valid both for religiousness and religion; we have religious feelings, emotions, and desires, but we should not have them without faith, and faith is judgement, reasoning, conviction—and so intellectual activity. Every belief in the last resort comes from reason, even if from imperfect and erroneous reason. Real faith is not a nail on which one could hang oneself in despair because of the weakness of reason——

nor opium for soothing the troubled soul.

Yes. Faith, true genuine faith that does not lull to sleep, but arouses and drives.

You spoke about tolerance; the need for tolerance in itself already means that there never will be one shepherd, and one fold.

One shepherd—perhaps, one fold, not so

readily. For the natural diversity of mankind; tell me, how many Christian churches and sects were there, and are there, how many interpretations of the Scriptures, and of Jesus' teaching, from the beginnings of Christianity to the present day—and how many dissensions are there also in scientific views! I have my own interpretation and my convictions; but I acknowledge the equal right of my neighbours, and therefore I do not bother their consciences and I become used to being tolerant. Tolerance, I repeat, is a positive virtue, and it is a new virtue, only proclaimed by true Christianity. By genuine tolerance the universal sheep-fold is being built, internationalism and pacifism are also striving for it. It is the continuation in the way that religion marked out.

People say—the modern religious crisis. Well yes, ecclesiastical religions all and everywhere are losing and have lost their influence. Science is finding itself more and more in conflict with the teaching of theology—this does not mean to say that in the Bible and in theology there are not enough true concepts particularly those dealing with religion and religiousness. But how comes it, then, that in spite of these quakings in their faith the majority of men remain in the churches? In that I also see the recognition of the value and need of religion.

Religion today must have a different function from what it used to have before. In those days the big mass of people was uneducated, ignorant, illiterate; therefore it was accustomed to docility —spiritually and politically authority ruled. The church as a spiritual aristocracy was the model of the political aristocracy; because of that it was also organized as a hierarchy—aristocracy is nothing but the acknowledgement of degrees among men. Today almost every man has some sort of education; in this way he is also more autonomous. Religion on the one hand must come to terms with this development of scientific thought, on the other with the development of social conditions—and not only in its doctrine. Also Christian love of one's neighbour has in front of it a tremendous task: the just claims of socialism.

VII

POLITICS

1. *Political Theory and Practice*

YOU say that the law of love is equally valid for politics and for personal life.

Of course, it is; isn't it valid for the whole of life, for all deeds and actions. All sensible and honest politics are the performing and strengthening of humanity within and without; politics, like everything else that we do, must be subject to ethical laws. I know that there are politicians, chiefly those who consider themselves to be terribly practical and clever, who do not care for that demand; but experience, not only mine, I think, shows that sensible and honest politics, as Havlíček says, are the most effective and most practical. In the end the ones that we call idealists are always right, and they do for the state, for the nation, and for mankind more than those politicians, that are said to be realistic and clever. The smart fellows are stupid in the long run.

Except that in their own time the idealists are not usually right.

Sometimes they are not, sometimes they are:

in politics too God's mills grind slowly, but they grind very fine. If I speak of morality in politics I am thinking in the first place of political tactics, and of administration as a whole; political practice itself must be moral—of course, the political programme also is subject to ethics. In the same way as the life of the individual and of society I cannot conceive of politics except sub specie aeternitatis.

Of course, anyone can write a political programme that is respectable enough, and even high principled. It is something different to know the administration, and to carry it out decently; and again it is something else to understand what, at some given time, is in the interest of the state and of the nation, in difficult and fateful moments to point the way, to decide upon suitable progress —and to lead. In this sense one speaks of higher politics, and one distinguishes between a statesman and a politician, or a party man; Palacký, Rieger, as the highest political authorities, were called leaders, and fathers of the nation. Conceived in this way politics constitute an attempt to grasp the given moment in the flow of history —a politician must know the history of his nation and state, he will understand its present, he will keep in mind its future.

I have lived through it all. As I have said, I

am a man of politics, political problems have interested and held me from my youth; you know that as early as 1891 I was a deputy, that I gave up the mandate, and the reason why. The conflicts of the time were for me merely the occasion, the true motive was my political immaturity. When I became acquainted with the politics of Vienna, and its relations with Europe, I also discovered that for such political life, in spite of all my training up till then, I was not yet properly prepared. I began my political studies afresh, and more thoroughly. I tried to clear up in my mind what really was the problem in our history; and the history of our nation was to me a part of world history. Besides that, social questions, the Slav question, and so on—I did not engage in practical politics, but I wrote books; and that also is political work.

At that time you also used to stress the point that politics should be scientific. Today after so much experience do you still adhere to this conception of politics?

Yes—politics are and always will be more of a science. In our universities, it is true, we do not yet possess any professors of politics; politics as a science are bandied about in the legal sections —political science, national and international law, statistics, political economics, and so on, and in the philosophical ones—history, sociology, and other sections. In other countries there are already special chairs and high educational posts for the science of politics, they also possess an extensive expert literature—it is true, even that is only a beginning; we have a long way to go yet to the science of politics.

Does it appear to you that there is a yawning chasm between scientific and practical, say parliamentary politics?

There is; how could it not be yawning? But there is the same chasm between the religious views of the masses of church-goers and of intelligent theologians; no less is the difference between the laymen and lawyers, and so on. But theology is not yet religion or religiousness, all jurisprudence is not yet law, legal consciousness and action; if I ask for theoretical, scientific politics, I do not forget the difference between theory and practice. Do look at our political development since the revolution; surely it is a striking thing that at the head of the government, of parliament, and of the parties with few exceptions there have been and still are men without any academic schooling, men who created, organized, and led the parties, who had a long and harsh training. These leaders and creators of the parties must in practice, and through practice, create a theory, without theory there is no practice. You know yourself how Švehla loved to theorize—and what a practical man he was! Our parties have their theories of socialism, or agrarianism, their philosophy of history, their conception of life, and so on. No, sir, without political education, without theoretical preparation, proper, I should say great politics are impossible. Well, yes: a pile of certificates is still no guarantee of education, and by no means do they replace natural talents. And don't forget the moral claim; book learning, examinations for titles and degrees are no guarantee of decency, honour, or courage.

And now a question—it ought not to be personal: when you speak of politics as a science, of educated politics, what is the relation of politics to philosophy?

You do not want to be personal but you are; you mean that from being a professor I became President? Well then impersonally:

Remember Plato, Aristotle, Augustine, Thomas Aquinas, and so on; the philosophers always were greatly concerned with political problems, political theory in some kind of form has always been part of philosophy. That is a consequence of the relation of politics to ethics; ethics always formed part of philosophy. In modern times sociology and the philosophy of history have crystallized out of philosophy, these are political sciences in the narrower sense of the word; in this way politics became an applied science. Today in addition to the philosophers, the lawyers, national economists, historians, and students of social science are working for the science of politics— every science has leanings on one side towards philosophy, on the other towards practical life.

Philosophy is in direct relation to politics, firstly by working for a general conception of life and of the world, and so also of social life. Today politics and the modern state comprise all branches of social administration, and so in practical ways they are striving for what philosophy does theoretically. It is in this sense that Plato's demand should be understood that philosophers should be rulers. As well as striving to achieve a general conception of life and of the world philosophy tries to attain to the principal fundamental truths of all action and knowledge, it desires certainty—a statesman concerned with so many disputes must continually decide where truth is. A modern statesman must be critical, he must be educated, and wise.

And not only wise. Politics demand a considerable degree of imagination: to penetrate into the minds of contemporary men, and into history as well, to anticipate the line of social development; and to visualize the ideal towards which that development is pointing—in short, a touch of poetry does the statesman no harm, but that is imagination, not phantasy, or a Utopia.

A politician, if he is to lead, requires a knowledge of men—what leadership is it if he cannot see into people? Let us, please, not forget that the scientist and philosopher also can make mistakes, and big mistakes. There are in fact politicians and politicians, just as there are scientists and scientists. And I repeat—books, certificates are not enough, a man of politics needs experience of life; nor is cleverness enough—as in all things, in politics also it is the worth of the whole man that matters.

2 . *History and the World*

You emphasize the significance of history for politics; apparently you have in mind the old vitae magistra.

Yes, after all, you know that I used to have frequent discussions and disputes on the substance of history; I was always interested in the lessons for our politics that follow from history, from our own and from that of the world. I do not presume to be a historian; but as a believer in teleology I try to grasp the sense of the world and of our actions——how much already have I racked my brains because of that! I seek for information from the historians, but I also observe what is happening at home, and outside——sir, in the course of more than half a century one sees much, and one has something to think about. I think that in the War I proved that I have a little of that historical sense. Well I kept proclaiming this again and again: that our politics must be cosmopolitan, with an international orientation. This follows from our history——and, from our tradition: even Palacky pointed out for us "cosmopolitan centralization."

Yes, but that axiom can also be proved geographically, in that we are a small nation and state, wedged in the middle of the Continent, on the watershed of natural spheres, races, cultures, and religions: therefore that we are necessarily the crossroads of Europe.

Yes, this is also important; but other states differently situated also have their problem of international orientation——in fact all states. Where there are frontiers, there are also neighbours, it is there that the other world begins. Whether we want to or not, we live politically in the world, and with the whole world. On all grounds only world politics are reasonable and permanent.

Doesn't that lead to the opinion that foreign politics are of greater importance than internal politics?

Not necessarily; sometimes foreign, sometimes internal politics are of greater importance for the state; in the long run foreign politics will always correspond in nations with the tone of internal affairs. With regard to our politics, that terrific world revolution caused by the Great War—and it was from that revolution that our freedom arose—makes it obligatory for us to become politically conscious of what in a historical sense it was all about; and where further development is pointing to.

I conceive of world politics in a realistic sense: that is, they must be based on the study of the world and of its history; we must become conscious of what is going on in the world, and what connects us with it. Don't get frightened, I am not going to start from the first Adam; neither shall we entertain ourselves with the history of the whole world; Europe is enough for us, and those neighbouring parts of Asia and Africa which developed historically in close association with Europe.

After all, Europe is a peninsula of Asia; and the history of Asia falls into that part that is nearest to Europe, so about as far as the frontiers of India and China; India, China with Japan, separated by high mountains and deserts from the western part of Asia had their own special cultural life.

165

After all, the frontiers that you give are roughly the frontiers of the white races.

Yes, roughly. Let us leave aside that real Asiatic Asia; European Asia and Asiatic Europe are sufficient for us. Those countries from the frontiers of India right to modern Portugal, the whole orbis terrarum round the Mediterranean Sea, together with Northern Africa, were from primeval times, and still are in close cultural contact; it was on this part of the earth that cultural syncretism originated, of language and of population. As Kollár would say, in this region there was sufficient intimate reciprocity, particularly of culture, and with it the mingling of races, and of nations.

It is a strange phenomenon that it was here that from the earliest times great world empires as we may call them arose. Thus one after the other came the Babylonian, Assyrian, Persian, as well as the Egyptian empires; the Greeks crumbled up into various tribes, but the Athenians made an attempt to unite Hellas into a single state after they had succeeded in driving off the aggressive Persians. With Alexander a huge world empire came into being, embracing Greece, Egypt, and the whole of the then known Asiatic East, as far as India; after Alexander his empire fell to pieces politically, but not in a cultural sense. This Greek culture, Hellenism, also spread to Rome, and further west, after Alexander the Roman world empire was set up. Rome, Italian in substance, embodied in itself Greece, Egypt, and northern Africa, in the East the nations and states of Alexander's empire, in West the Iberians, Celts, and Germans. The Roman empire fell into a western and an eastern part; the eastern part —Byzantium—survived the breaking up of the western one. Further world empires arose in the West: Frankish, Germano-Roman, Spanish, Austrian——

And the empire of Islam. And the Swedish attempt to subjugate the North.

Yes. And in more recent times: Napoleon's France, the growth of England as a colonial world-empire, the rise of the federal North American state, the rise of Russia as an Eurasian realm, the union of Italy, and her desire to dominate the Mediterranean, the growth of Prussia, and of the new German empire, modern Japan—in short, everywhere and at all times you have that historical process of the formation of great world empires.

That peculiar urge for political power is also manifest in the smaller states; our old Bohemian state was for a certain time in a relative sense a world power, the same may be said of Poland,

Bulgaria, Serbia—well everywhere, and at all times you meet with that urge; to extend beyond its frontiers, to organize within itself other nations and other states.

For the rise of the great empires geographical factors were of considerable significance: mountains, the river highways—the Nile, Danube, Rhine—and chiefly the sea. For the West the Mediterranean was of special political importance —its name alone indicates what significance it had in binding together the nations' settled on its shores, particularly the Greeks, Romans, Phoenicians. Even Plato grasped the value of this sea at that time. There was also a tendency in the Eastern states in its direction: Babylonia, Assyria, Persia, and Egypt too.

It is only in more recent times that progress in seamanship opened up the Atlantic Ocean— the connection between Europe and America; for today and for the future the Pacific Ocean is increasing in importance—the connection between America and the Far East. China, Japan and India across the sea become the neighbours of Europe and America.

Those great empires—we call them great powers—arose mainly from political action, from the urge to domineer and the eagerness for conquest, from the subjugation of one state by another, of one nation by another; sometimes over-population and hunger lead to conquest—bona terra, mali vicini. In a national sense these great states used to be bi-national and multi-national, and they were controlled by the dominant race. And because mutual understanding was necessary among individuals, and among nations of different languages, the language of communication and of the state arose. In olden times there was no modern nationalistic feeling; with foreign rule the language was also accepted —through the administration, the army, commerce, religion and culture. With the world empires world languages also developed. It was not only political supremacy that led to this, but also the need for culture, and so the foreign languages of nations of a higher culture were accepted. From the beginning culture was the connecting link between nations and states, and cultural reciprocity developed. And the spirit reached further than the sword.

The first great cultural power, I should say, was Greece. You must realize the special position of the ancient Greeks: they were to an equal degree a nation of Europe and of Asia Minor, and, therefore, from the earliest times they were the mediators between Europe and Asia; they had settlements also in Southern Italy, in Egypt, in Cyrenaica, and they had their emporia throughout the whole Mediterranean. Still earlier than Hellenistic culture the oldest Eurasian culture was Aegean, Creto-Mycenian, and also Greek; there was, therefore, an older connection than history itself.

During the period of the flowering of their culture the Greeks had a profound influence on the nations of the Old World; in the time of Alexander, and after him, Greek became the universal language in Europe, Asia, Africa; in a cultural sense it also conquered the imperial Romans, and with them it was de facto the second state language. I have treasured in my mind the advice of the Roman poet: Vos exemplaria graeca nocturna versate manu, versata diurna. It is obvious that even then culture had a supernational, cosmopolitan validity.

You find the same with Latin down to the Middle Ages, with French in modern times, with English. It is evident that relations between nations are not only a question of political power, not only of the sword, the spirit also conquers the world; the exchange of natural and industrial goods leads to commerce—again another aspect of cosmopolitan reciprocity. It has been like this since the beginning.

Well, look at the unending historical process,

what it means: nations and states cannot live in isolation, besides their internal organization they strive for organization among themselves, for associations between states and between nations. Mankind gradually organizes itself as a whole; the history of conquests, empires, cultures and languages shows us that. For us, the last phase of this development was the World War, and the post-War period.

The question is: should this organization of states, nations, and continents come about through violence, that is, through conquest, subjugation, or, as one says today, in the imperialistic way, or peacefully, by federation, by political, economic, and cultural agreements required for the purpose? The programme for the peaceful world organization was drawn up after the War by the League of Nations, by working for Pan-Europe, and by hundreds of associations and movements for rapprochement between nations. We may say that we stand only on the threshold of the true cosmopolitan organization.

I have grown somewhat talkative; but that glance back into the past says much for our time, for us, for our state and nation.

Don't put yourself out, I can see what you are making for.

Gratias for patience; yes, there is something

from which to learn. In the first place we may again and fully appreciate Kollár's idea of reciprocity, and Palacký's idea of cosmopolitan centralization, from knowledge of that Palacký drew up for us his political programme. It pleases me that already our first pioneers, our first cultural leaders grasped and proclaimed that idea at such an early stage. We might call it part of our political tradition.

The development of mankind really appears, and in the full meaning of the word, as the development of reciprocity, of syncretism of culture, language, and population. At the very beginning of historical development while there was no stronger and more extensive organization of the state this syncretism occurred among neighbouring tribes, spread so to speak from one village to the next; then the original tribal organization grew out into the state organization, and as time went on some states acquired political supremacy over neighbouring ones—world powers arose.

Hand in hand with the political relations between nations, the syncretism of culture and population developed. The cultures mingled, the races and nations also mingled. This mingling of the races we can trace everywhere, with us as in other places. There isn't such a thing as what is called pure blood—we have not got it, we are not pure-blooded Slavs, just as neither the Germans, Frenchmen, or Englishmen and so on have got it. Nobody, nowhere. All that talk about some pure, or superior race is a political myth. Europeanism and Europism arose just from that very mixing, just by that mutual enrichment of the blood and of the spirit.

Equally widely spread is cultural syncretism, and by it also that of language. You have examples enough—take English, French, Italian, Spanish, or any other language. The influence of German on us, Germanisms in our language. It is not only a question of mutual verbal influences, of taking over and translating individual words, but also the influence of syntax, and of what is called the spirit of the language. Nations learned from one another, nothing can prevent this. A fine example is how the Gauls and Germans learned from the Romans, although they were fighting against them all the time; but people acquire knowledge even in the conflict with their opponents, for conflict, even a physical one, is de facto also reciprocity.

And cultural reciprocity—those gifted Greeks already learned from the Orient, the imperial Romans from the Greeks; and their culture survives to the present day. To the present day their poets and historians are being read, Roman law is being studied, the whole of European culture stands on foundations of the ancient world. Not only the Renaissance and Humanism, already the medieval church continued in that culture, it preserved its language, art, philosophy—that is one of the finest examples in history. Not the sword, but the spirit. A man does not live on bread alone, nations do not live on bread alone. I do not believe in the omnipotence of political violence.

Further lessons: that the racial and national minorities have existed from the very earliest development of mankind. De facto, every European state contains within itself linguistic minorities; small states, and nations are minorities among the bigger states, and nations, and even the greatest states and nations in the last resort are a minority in comparison with the whole of mankind. Therefore, a proper solution of the political problem of minorities is the presupposition of a better, and more cosmopolitan organization in the world.

A bit of cosmopolitism and polyglotism is part of the trousseau of modern man. To know other nations so as to appreciate better the quality and individuality of one's own. To praise one's own nation merely because the others are foreign and unknown to us, that I should say is blind love. Of course: we shall not ape other nations. Cultural internationalism does not exclude the intimate love of one's own nation, nor the desire to preserve its cultural autonomy.

As evidence of that: how a nation so universal and cosmopolitan as the English could respect and preserve its essential character.

Yes, that's it: with cosmopolitism to preserve one's own. And a further great lesson from history; culture, education is a powerful political force, is more permanent than the state, army, and economic power. I don't know of worse faint-heartedness than the present talk about the decline of European culture. If it does decline then only to pass into cosmopolitan culture.

And what then is the meaning of the League of Nations, the movement for Pan-Europa and all those organizations? We already have several hundreds of international and universal scientific, legal, social institutions, and so on—yes, even sport today is cosmopolitan. It is obvious that the nations are beginning to understand the most important fact that the reciprocity required can be achieved by mild and reasonable means, not through violence, through federation, the organization of independent states and nations. The World War was also a federation of two great groups—today the problem is to assist in the conciliation and unification of the continents, and of the whole of mankind. It won't all happen at once, and easily, hardly any one of us will live to witness perfect unification; but again I am referring to those mills of God's.

I remember what Napoleon came to on St. Helena: that in Europe there would no longer be any other arrangement possible except a league of nations. According to him, he was compelled to subdue Europe with arms, but now it had to be persuaded; there were no reasons for keeping hatred alive among the nations. Well I wonder: how many Napoleons and little Napoleons will have still to come to reason?

Reciprocity, internationalism, cosmopolitanism—we have a more comprehensive word for it: humanity. The development of the world is working towards universal humanity, to pure humanism, as Kollár called it, and as Palacký believed.

3. History and Ourselves

And then: can a nation as small as we are intervene more strongly in what is going on in the world?

It can; in our history itself you will find plenty

of instances of that; just have a good look at it! I told you that from it I learned about politics theoretically and practically. I occupied myself constantly with our history; all the same I wrote against historicism, against the exaggeration of the glories of the past. What is called the present is also history; not the process itself but the things that are developing should be the object of our study—hence "realism." Whether the historian wishes to or not he proceeds into the past from that present with which and in which he lives. What concerned me always was the philosophy of history, for me the problem is the meaning of our European and world development as a whole. But enough has been said about all that.

I need not concern myself with the questions whence and when we came into our land; our national life begins in the Seventh Century; like the Germans and the rest we were divided into various spheres. Politically and culturally we were more backward than states to the west, and, therefore, dependent on them. The Roman influence naturally exerted its greatest influence in the Romanesque countries; also the Germans had already lived for several hundred years before us under the Roman influence, and in the Tenth Century they were so far advanced that they could revive the Roman Empire. Our origin and development were different; and so also in literature Humanism with us did not penetrate so far as with the Germans, who had been previously and more strongly involved in the universal Roman culture.

Our state from the earliest times under the wise guidance of the Přemyslids formed a part of the resuscitated Roman Empire; it is a problem for our historians to give a proper explanation of the relation of our lands to the German Empire. At one time our kings themselves became Roman-German emperors—our relation to the Medieval Roman Empire at that time was intimate enough; I mention this in order to emphasize the political influence of Rome also on us. Our kings attempted through conquest and dynastic politics to create in the middle of Europe a more powerful state organization; Břetislav I, Venceslas II, Přemysl Otakar II, and the Luxemburgs maintained an imperialism of its kind, our realm then extended for a time as far as Krakovia and Posen, Hungary, Styria, and Carinthia, Lousnitz, Brandenburg. One can see from that that even then people were aware of the problem of Central Europe, and at times it was being tackled in a political sense with energy enough. Politics then were in the right sense European, politics in which the question was to the same extent our wider association with Europe as a whole, as well as our security on the exposed crossroads between the East and West, North and South. That European conception had its ups and downs; it reached its climax in Charles's time when the Czech royal dynasty assumed control of the Roman Empire, and when our nation in a cultural sense attached itself more closely to the West—the golden age of our Gothic.

King Jiří was well aware of our political situation in the middle of Europe when a peaceful association·of Christian rulers was in his mind— a medieval anticipation of the League of Nations. You have only to steep yourself in our history— you will find in it that it was not only a question of local events but of international ones as well.

Our religious development has been similar. The introduction and spread of Christianity has with us, as it had everywhere else, a tremendous cultural significance. The medieval church also was our teacher and leader; the influence of Byzantium was not permanent, very soon and rightly·we decided for the West. Altogether one must understand that in the Middle Ages the church as well as the state was the political leader and organizer of society. The Middle Ages were simply theocratic.

Just as Catholicism reached us from the West,

from Germany, the impulse of the Reformation also came to us from the West, from England: Wyclif—Hus. As early as the Thirteenth Century, it is true, attempts had been made to reform the morals of the church, but our nation embarked on a wider and deeper reform, just as a whole nation. On the value of our reformation by the Hussites and the Brethren I accept the opinion of Palacký. Our Hussite movement opened up the way for reformations in other countries; Luther correctly described himself as a Hussite. The reformation of our church was really an international movement.

Then you have the Counter-Reformation: this also had a European and international significance. The Thirty Years War swept away our political independence, and roughly stabilized Europe for centuries. The Roman church was compelled by the revolution of the Reformation to formulate its teaching more precisely at the Council. of Trent; it had itself to carry out reforms; special attention began to be given to education, schools, and cultural enlightenment. Our Komenský represents the climax of our Reformation

Through the discovery of ocean routes Europe, until that time turned towards Asia, began the movement to the West, and gradually it mastered the whole world. In this way new international

forces and political groupings arose. This development, our intimate relation to the German-Roman
Empire, our Reformation and the Counter-
Reformation begot Austria; the union of Austria,
Bohemia, and Hungary was not brought about
without our active participation—Austria did not
spring up overnight. And it did not arise merely
for defence against the Turks; it was neither the
first nor the last solution of the problem of Central
Europe.

Austria, not without the help of our own people,
carried through the Counter-Reformation with
violence; it suppressed the Czech reformation,
weakened and destroyed our political independence; for us the period of decadence began. A
strange dispensation: so that Austria could re-
Catholicize the nation it deprived it of nobility,
and leaders; in this way it created a nation that
in kernel and substance was democratic, one that
at the first opportunity of its own self threw off
the yoke of absolutism and of monarchy. Historical
justice!

The religious Reformation and the Counter-
Reformation, the Renaissance and Humanism,
then the growth of science and of the new
philosophy, led in Europe to restlessness and a
revolutionary spirit; from them Enlightenment,
essentially anti-religious, and the French Revolu-

tion took their origin. Enlightenment, especially of the French and Germans, provided the cultural basis for our national revival; just remember the significance that the advancement of education and of culture in general had for the leaders of the nation. You have Dobrovský, Šafařík, Kollar, Palacký, Havlíček, and so on. And in that revival of ours there is again a strong Western element, of that new cosmopolitism; with our new national consciousness there was associated the conception of reciprocity, chiefly of Slavism—Kollár; Palacký refers to cosmopolitan centralization—our national revival at the same time was a democratic and cosmopolitan revival.

The revolution—the great one, and the other smaller revolutions too—awakened us politically; even if we could take active part in them only to a small extent, our political ideas are derived from them.

That is also shown by the fact that nearly all our political movements and plans since 1918 had already found expression with us in 1848: the expropriation of the big estates, social reforms, a national church, equal rights for women, and so on.

Yes. The year 1848 also gave birth to the first political movements and parties. The time was coming for a constitutional régime, of course after the Viennese model: after the doubtful experiment

of political abstinence—we were not prepared
well enough for active politics, and so we discovered for ourselves the apron of abstinence—
we decided upon active politics, for competition
with the Germans and the Hungarians in the
parliamentary and senatorial tiltyard at the time
when the European conflagration was being
prepared.

In the World War we gained our political
independence; but the War was not warfare alone,
it was also a world revolution; it destroyed three
empires, the three last great strongholds of absolutism; the world drew nearer to democracy. The
fact that in some states a reaction and the
enthronement of absolutism in this or that form
has come about, that cannot mislead us; the old
régime gives place to the new one step by step,
and step by step the new régime develops;
democracy is still in its swaddling clothes.

This, then, in a nutshell is our Czech and
Slovak development with regard to politics. You
see that in it from the beginning forces decided
—and at times also originated—that influenced
world events. A small nation, yes; but our globe
is also small, and yet it is subject to cosmic
forces.

4. *From Theocracy to Democracy*

You said that the World War was also a world revolution. Do you think that that world revolution is to be one of the last?

There have always been revolutions: but the present is almost a permanent revolution. Remember, apart from the revolution of the Reformation, the Dutch fight for freedom, the English rebellion, the American revolt, and particularly the great French Revolution. The wars against Napoleon represented the counter-revolutionary reaction for the suppression of the principles of the French Revolution; against this reaction the revolutions of the years 1830, 1848, and so on, broke out. In revolutionizing Europe, Italy holds a prominent place. In fact, we live in a revolutionary century; revolution almost became a habit. The World War was the child of this movement of revolt, and it itself was a great revolution. I have lived long enough to witness many revolutions in politics, but also in culture, literature, and in other things; the modern spirit of revolt is not limited to the political field: political upheavals to a large extent are provoked by revolutionary ideas.

Whether the world revolution is the last—I should like it to be, and according to the world as a whole that might be possible. It is a tremendous political achievement that the nations at Geneva and elsewhere are continually having conferences about urgent problems. That people are not patient enough when this great work—one of the greatest—is not an immediate success, in that I see one of the political failings of the time—and a rather potent legacy of the spirit of the ancient régime.

I repeat: revolutions—I mean bloody revolutions—will be superfluous, as soon as we abolish the oppression of one nation by another, of one class by another, and the dominion by force of some over the souls of others. Revolutions may cease, but the spirit of revolution will persist. Don't we speak of revolutionary discoveries, and isn't every great new thought, in its way, a revolution?

The natural sciences also agree with that; they show that progress does not only take place by gradual changes, but also by jumps, mutations—in short, by revolutions.

Yes. The Reformation was a revolution—a religious revolution; but because religion is the moral leader of the individual and of society, it was also a social and political revolution. Catholic states, because they have not experienced such a strong religious and ecclesiastical revolution, are politically more revolutionary, and more radical; in them the conflict between ecclesiastical religion and anti-ecclesiastical enlightenment is the cause of a greater spiritual, and therefore also of a greater political tension. You see that in Orthodox Russia, and in the chronic revolutionary spirit of the Romanesque states; or in the difference between the temperament of the Protestant English and of the Catholic Irish. With us and in us the Catholic and Protestant, the radical and reforming temperaments are in conflict; that conflict you can also observe in our modern politics. Our politics are, and have been since our revival, essentially rationalistic, enlightened. In this we are like France—hence those natural sympathies with her.

You used to say that the Protestant countries are more democratic than the Catholic ones.

Well, yes. After all, Protestantism abolished the aristocratic priesthood and celibacy, it abolished the Catholic hierarchy; in this way it made the church and all social life democratic. Through reference to the Bible it led to the training of the members of the church and made them think; in matters of faith, by making the individual conscience the final appeal, it fostered individualism, subjectivism, personal freedom, and personal responsibility as against priestly and ecclesiastical authority. By all this Protestantism prepared the ground for political democracy.

Would you also say today that the Protestant countries are more democratic?

I know what is in your mind; but we must wait for their further development. When I speak of the Protestant countries I mean those that I know well: England, America. After all, England with its parliamentary system and America with its declaration of human rights are teachers of democracy.

And what about France?

France carried out its reformation too, but politically—through enlightenment and revolution. Positivism is the child of France, and French politics and economics are directed by that Positivism; you can see that in its capitalism. Modern capitalism, industrialism, and the bourgeoisie developed, surely, first and furthest in the Protestant countries, especially in the Calvinistic and Puritanical ones. Under the influence of Max Weber this is continually being discussed. The whole system and spirit of Protestantism by weakening attachment to the miraculous and sacramentalism, and by fostering individual initiative, led to the recognition of personal achievement and of commonplace work. Modern capitalism and democracy developed simultaneously and from the same source. And both again are associated with modern science and philosophy—it is no accident that modern scientific and philosophical tendencies are more vigorous in the Protestant countries. National economy as a science also developed most effectively in England. It is no accident that in England Marxian socialism matured scientifically, different from French or Russian socialism; the latter is more political, more Utopian, the former is founded on scientific lines. In the end —under the influence of England—and contrary to the radicalism of the revolutionary year 1848, Marx and Engels admitted that parliamentary tactics are preferable. Lenin stuck more firmly to the younger, unfermented, more revolutionary Marx, and with him to Bakunin than to the older and more mature Marx.

Of course, I am not setting Catholicism and Protestantism in sharp contrast to each other. Surely in the conflict of the Reformation, Catholicism reformed itself, and since that time between these two Christian movements there have been strong mutual ties—ties of dispute, but all the more effective. I only wish again to emphasize that deep relation that exists between religion and politics, the church and the state. In spiritual matters the church led society and in this way it also led the state; on the other hand the state protected rights and laws which in substance are founded on morality and therefore also on religion. Catholicism by its magnificent ecclesiastical organization established the highest type of theocracy, the Papo-Caesarism. Orthodoxy was Caesaro-Papistic, as was the Reformation and the Counter-Reformation—this is expressed in the principle cuius regio eius religio. The modern state becomes more and more secularized, it takes over the control of the whole social organization; at first absolute and authoritative, as theocracy was, it passes over more and more into a constitutional, semi-democratic, and democratic régime. In this way, then, democracy, the modern state, is the successor of the theocratic regime. Theocracy derives all state and political power from the Divine Will, democracy from the people; the people and the parliament elected by it are the source of all power, and the highest political authority. But don't forget that even the Schoolmen acknowledged the political power of the people, and that there were Catholic and Protestant lawyers and theologians who proclaimed the right to rebel and to put down tyrants.

Don't you think that religion tends more towards monarchism than to democracy?

Religion no, but theocracy yes. Did not monarchism put forward its claim that it was by divine

grace? Monarchism is a state form of aristocratism—and there was not only a political form
of aristocratism but also a religious one: hierarchy. The aristocrat says: I master—you servant,
or slave; the democrat says: I master—you
master. The teaching of Jesus, the doctrine of
love towards one's neighbour, and general equality
is certainly not aristocratic, on the contrary. For
me, from love of one's neighbour, from divine
sonship follows democracy, I should say, of the
right kind.

5. Democracy

*What, then, would you give us as your own and
the strongest argument for democracy?*

The strongest argument for democracy—faith
in man, in his spirit and immortal soul; that is
true, metaphysical equality. Ethically democracy
is based on the political realization of love of one's
neighbour. The eternal to the eternal cannot be
indifferent, the eternal cannot misuse the eternal,
it cannot exploit and violate it.

*Then in the end you see the true foundation of
democracy in religion; if I may say so, you are really
a theocrat.*

I am not frightened of words, and I have
nothing against that expression if you take theo-

cracy literally as the rule of God. I conceive the state, national life, politics, like the whole of life, in truth sub specie aeternitatis. True democracy founded on love and respect for one's neighbour, and towards all neighbours, is the realization of the rule of God on earth.

Democracy is not only a form of government, it is not only what is written in constitutions; democracy is a view of life, rests on faith in men, in humanity and in human nature, and there is no faith without love, there is no love without faith. I said once that democracy is a discussion. But real discussion is only possible where men trust one another, and honestly seek the truth. Democracy is a conversation among equals, the thinking of free people open to complete publicity—the word "parliament" has a fine meaning, if only we could give it body!

I said among equals. I know that men are not equal; nowhere on the earth or in Nature is there equality—there is variety; only as immortal souls are we really equivalent. Liberté, egalité, fraternité—even the French Revolution de facto accepted Jesus' commandment, the commandment of love towards one's neighbour. It sounds like a paradox, but it is true: the French revolutionaries were theocrats, even if they had God merely as a Highest Being.

The democratic ideal is not only political, it is social and economic. Communism I reject. Without individualism, without gifted and inventive individuals, without capable leaders, without geniuses society cannot be reasonably and justly organized. Democracy on its social side means the abolition of degrading misery; in a republic, in a democracy, it must not be possible for individuals or ranks to exploit their co-citizens— in a democracy man to a man must not be merely a means. The natural variety must be organized through the division and gradation of functions and work; no organization of men is possible without superiors and subordinates, but it must just be an organization, and not privilege, not aristocratic coercion but mutual service. Democracy needs leaders, not masters.

I accept democracy also with its economic and material consequences; but I base it on love— on love and the justice that is the mathematics of love, and on the conviction that we should help in the world towards the realization of the rule of God, towards synergism with the divine will.

I know the principles of democracy nowadays are often taken from materialism; materialism no doubt has been refuted by science—just look at those modern sciences, what they have to say on the matter—but it persists in the overvaluation of the material conditions of life. I know there was, and still is, material oppression, but that is only a part of spiritual oppression. The objection is brought against theism that faith in immortality and the love of one's neighbour is content with philanthropy, with alms, that it does not lead to the modern socialistic demand for the legal and judicial abolition of misery. I don't know why it should not. Theism, religion as a whole, after all, is not merely a personal attitude, it is a collective order, and it strives everywhere and always to become an organization. Reasonable love, religion directed by reason will bring about humanity through law, but it will never deprive us of the moral obligations of personal participation and assistance. Altogether it would be a strange democracy if there were no place for moral individual initiative.

You speak of perfect democracy; nowadays it is more the custom to look for its failings, and to talk about the crisis of democracy.

The crisis of democracy—tell me where isn't there a crisis today? We are simply living in a period of transition: as you know, Švehla used to say that the War is still going on, even if there is no shooting. We are—all nations and states are—in a difficult regeneration; it is not easy to ask for perfection that would last for ever. This does not mean that our democracy, our arrangements as a whole, could not be better than they are. Democracy has its faults because the citizens have their faults. The shop is like its master.

Look at us: For centuries we had not our own dynasty, we did not have—but for minor exceptions—a nationally conscious aristocracy, we had no rich, and big gentlemen—in virtue of our history and nature, we are destined for democracy. Culturally we belong to Western Europe; again a reference to enlightened democracy. We are a nation democratic in body and soul; if our democracy has its shortcomings, we must overcome these shortcomings, but not overcome democracy.

For instance, people say: parliament is no longer sufficient. Not NO LONGER but NOT YET: parliament is elected by the constituencies—what has given these constituencies their political and moral education? The old régime; we still do not possess deputies who grew up during the Republic. Democracy must not only exist in the statute book, and in the mouths of demagogues. Not even the best parliament exists to vote for what is truth, right, and morality; you cannot take a majority vote about truth, the fundamental

194

principles of politics, about right and morality.
Democracy alone does not bring up people.
Decent, real people are brought up by the family,
schools, churches, the government, literature,
journalism, and so on—does democracy prevent
that? Isn't there a vicious political circle here?
Democracy is made by democrats, and better
democracy by better democrats. Only let us admit
that the so-called intelligentsia bears its share of
guilt—the clergy, the teachers, writers, officials,
and people as a whole who train and teach the
mass of the citizens. Democracy is guided by the
majority—who and what then are these leaders
like? A French writer recently pointed clearly to
the "trahison des clercs."

People complain of corruption—well for it!
But don't let us be misled by generalizations—
and don't let us believe the corrupters who complain of corruption. There is plenty of silent
corruption, of that clever evasion of laws, almost
legal corruption—it is not enough to combat this
negatively, but positively; more respect for the
laws and the state! Yes, I am thinking of civilian
morality—loyalty in the English sense.

To the same extent as with corruption, people
complain of political faults, of the incapacity of
the deputies, of the government, and of all kinds
of public servants. Yes, we make mistakes, I

myself have made enough of them, we have not learned our lesson yet. The Republic, democracy, our state is young, and was given to us almost for nothing. We have no tradition in politics, and in administration, and therefore we make mistakes.

I am not speaking against criticism, on the contrary, I desire the criticism of all faults and mistakes; but that criticism should not be for the demagogy, but for instruction and improvement. We need educated and honest critics who have the manliness and courage of citizens; true criticism is not negation, not putting responsibility on others, but co-operation and co-responsibility.

People complain of the political parties. Rightly so in so far as these parties indulge in party selfishness. But the parties after all, are not and cannot be other than the average of their electors, this again depends upon the Press and upon the education of the citizens—always that problem of leadership! One thing we must always keep on demanding from the parties: that for their deputies and representatives they should select decent, politically capable, educated men and women. For me, politics and democracy are a tremendously serious matter: a task, I should say, for the best and carefully selected people.

And when we really take the amelioration of our affairs in hand we shall not forget the rising political generation—that is such an important problem for the state, for its government, and parties! The old problem of fathers and children! And again that vicious circle: are our clergy, teachers, writers, and journalists sufficiently alive to it? Do the government, parties, and deputies keep it in mind?

And what about the voices calling for the state of estates, or for a dictatorship?

Well you won't ask me to discuss the whole of political science; we simply set out from the existing political conditions, and said this and that towards the improvement of our public affairs. I know that even with us there are people who fix their eyes on the estate, or dictator states—

But only on the big and powerful ones; the smaller ones no longer provide such an attractive example.

Of course. People like power, but that power cannot be imitated; no régime will convert a small state into a great power. People think little of what suits us; they often merely ape what is foreign, instead of learning lessons from abroad —first of all to wait to see how it will turn out! Five years, ten years are still a short time for an historical argument. Well let us say: estates instead of parties, a state of estates? In the Middle Ages there was a state of estates everywhere—

197

tell me why the people did not keep it? Were the estates more unselfish than the present parties? And aren't the parties with us to a large extent estate parties? Today there are hundreds and hundreds of special occupations and estate interests —how do you intend to arrive at any agreement among them if not again by some sort of parliament? Dictators abolished parliament, but they appeal to the will of the people; so that in fact they make their appeal to democracy. And again: absolute monarchies were dictatorships of a kind —why didn't the people keep them?

Towards the end of the War I thought: it will be a republic in our case, but run at the beginning like a dictatorship. And you see, our republic could do without it. I am not afraid of words, and I maintain that even democracy is not without a certain degree of dictatorship; when parliament is not sitting the president and the government have unlimited power; but they are bound by laws and they are subject to future criticism, and to the control of parliament, to the criticism of the newspapers, and meetings. This also is the very foundation of democracy: free criticism, and public control.

On principle, but not blindly, I am a believer in democracy; I know the weak points of the system, and no bad experience has escaped me, but—not for a moment do I regret the decision to which I came when I was returning from the War: that I was going to serve the Republic and democracy.

Democracy is a guarantee of peace. For us and for the world.

VIII

NATION

1. *A Small Nation*

*Y*OU *said that in more recent times, besides the church and state, the nation has also emerged as the leading political factor.*

Yes, but rather late. Nationalism and socialism are the youngest political movements; therefore they are still so much in a ferment. In earlier times there were no nationalistic problems—the church with its universalism united all nations; the states were dynastic and territorial but not national. Admittedly, xenophobia existed—you find it already in our Dalimil; but conscious nationalism is solely a child of the last century. Today all the states in substance are national; today, at least in Europe, there is no longer a burning problem of free and unfree nations, but of great and small nations, of powerful and of numerically weaker states.

I know, with a nation quantity counts for much. The size of its army and the significance of it is obvious; economic power also depends on the number of workers. All work, physical and spiritual, can be better divided with a greater number of hands and brains; this influences the quantity and quality of production, the ability to compete, and so on. And finally the size of the country—also an excellent advantage.

But number without doubt is not always decisive. We have plenty of examples of smaller nations successfully confronting greater ones and defeating them; also in literature and in art, altogether in the whole sphere of cultural work, quality does not depend merely on numerical strength. One recalls the significance of the Italian towns, or of the German Hansa, of ancient Athens, the ancient Jews, and so on. The question has also been asked whether the smaller nations are happier; comparing Holland, Denmark and others with Russia, China, India But who can measure human happiness, and in what way?

In Europe there are five great powers of big nations, two of medium size, and nearly thirty are small; to put it in a nutshell: the point is, if the bigger ones will leave the smaller and tiny ones in peace! Even before the War the fate of the small nations appealed to me; for them I could see only one solution—political co-operation and reciprocity in economics and culture. During the War it was self-evident: if we were to gain our freedom, all the suppressed nations must gain theirs; the problem of the small nations was for me a cosmopolitan one. I should put it like this: big states and nations are cosmopolitan through their own power and size; the smaller nations must be cosmopolitan just because of their relative smallness and weakness. A good example of what I mean is the Little Entente, now today also the Balkan Entente, and others.

It is important to realize that the modern feeling of nationalism has grown up simultaneously with the feeling of internationalism. Nationality and internationality are not exclusive but they compensate each other. Nations are not threatened by internationalism but by other nationalism, as we call them, the aggressive ones. Modern internationalism, as represented by the League of Nations and other organizations, is a significant advantage on the very side of nationality.

Big and small nations—in the long run that is not laid down with immutable validity; the great ones with time can become relatively small, the small greater, until great. We have today promising beginnings to the scientific study of population; statistics put important information in the hands of government officials, statesmen, and historians. Even today politics and government cannot be carried on anyhow; we must bear in mind how many inhabitants, and of what kind, how many workers, how many unemployed, how many people can emigrate each year, and so on. We already feel that America does not admit our emigrants as she did before; we see in Italy, Japan, Germany how the fear of over-population exerts its effect. Today no statesman and government official can neglect the problem of population——the student of ethics, the clergy, and physicians are concerned with them as well. This is further proof that politics, whether people like it or not, must become scientific.

Before the War people used to reckon how many more separate nations there would be in fifty, a hundred years; the French were said to be a nation declining in numbers. Today statisticians, and the German ones in particular, show that the number of the German race is also already on the decline; Europe of the future, they say, will be mostly Slav. For us it is a matter of importance that in Slovakia the people will increase more rapidly than in the historical lands; our Germans are slightly less prolific than the Czechs. All this has considerable political significance for the near future, and foreseeing governments will bear it in mind.

Does the numerical increase of the Slavs justify the programme of the Pan-Slavs?

Beware of the word programme. Usually it

is terribly vague—even Neruda disliked "Slav twaddle." After all, there are so many disputes between the Slav nations; we have them too. Today all the Slav nations, except for the Lusatians, are free, first of all then, each of us will be concerned with the uplift of our own nation. As an independent state we shall work for friendship with the Slavs; to this we are also driven in that we have mutual opponents.

I do not underrate the emotional value of Slav reciprocity; but I look upon it as a step to wider, and the widest reciprocity. Besides Slav reciprocity Kollár already called for reciprocity also with the non-Slav nations!

2 *Love for One's Nation*

We often discuss the question of our national character. The Romantics used to speak of a dove-like nature; today we prefer to lay stress on the sober, practical features of our character. Well then, what are we really like?

It is difficult to say. I am sceptical of the current definitions as to what constitutes national character; and also of those that other nations give themselves. Was Žizka a true Czech, or Hus, Chelčický, and Komenský? Dobrovský,

Palacký, and Havlíček, or Hanka, and Jungman?
I have read a book by a Swiss author about a dual
France. Some people complain of our lack of
concord as if it were characteristically Czech, and
Slav, but the Germans complain about themselves
in exactly the same way. And so on. The problem
becomes more involved when we ask if and how
national character changes at different times, and
if there are some characteristic qualities that
remain unchanged. There is also the point that
from the earliest times until now there has been
a considerable mixing of races and nations. There
is no such thing as so-called "pure blood," at
least not in Europe.

And besides: how and to what extent do
economic conditions—prosperity, poverty, food,
and occupation, technique, culture, religion, and
morality, hygiene, and so on—form the national
character? On the other hand one has to consider,
how economic conditions, religion, and morality:
how culture in general is determined, and to what
extent by national character? For instance, is
mathematics influenced by the nation, have
French or English mathematics some special
character, and what is it? Is Catholicism intrinsi-
cally Roman, Protestantism German, and the
Orthodox Church Slav?

I won't deny that nations have their characters,

both physical, and spiritual, but I do not regard anthropological, and ethnological notions as already so certain that one could deduce from them the history of nations, and devise the right politics.

First of all, in our history nearly three hundred years are lacking of a full and free political and spiritual life; from that I would explain the immaturity in our politics; I do not deduce our shortcomings in politics from the character of the nation.

Secondly, as a society we are without traditions; the folk tradition of the peasantry is breaking up, and we have no other; almost every one of us has come from cottages, and we have not yet had time to get ourselves into shape.

And further: I ask you how long ago is it since the Moravians felt themselves to be something different from the Czechs, and talked of a Moravian "nation"? And now the Slovaks have been joined to us, and people speak of two nations. And it would not be only a question of the definition of the character of one nation but also of the character of the various parts of the country; what for instance is the difference between a Moravian Valach and a Hanak? Therefore I repeat: we lived in subjection, and each subjection prevents the character from developing and expanding fully according to its inner law.

That is also visible in our literature. Our poetry is good but not our novels and drama. For poetry personal life is sufficient; novels and drama presuppose the accumulated experience of generations; novels are a work of a whole century.

Yes——a small poem springing from a real strong impulse, many poets make a success of that. But that is just the expression of a peculiar personal feeling; the novel, and the drama are something different——an epical poem is too, they presuppose an artistic observation of the nation, society, classes, states, and so on. In our novels I take exception to some kind of unripeness, a restricted knowledge of one's own and foreign life, too little cosmopolitanism. We observe too little.

Foreigners say of us that we are talented, practical, industrious——well thank God too for that. In fact our farmers, our workers, are some of the best; the urban and intellectual strata are still incomplete, but we Czechs had not begun to urbanize ourselves until sixty or eighty years ago——I can still remember what modest beginnings they were, and I can say what a fair part of the way we have gone since then.

We need fifty years of undisturbed development, and we shall be where we should like to be today. It is no blind confidence in our ability, and tenacity——our history, even if somewhat disjointed, the fact that in the great political storms we held our ground, and that during the world conflagration we managed to restore our state, that all testifies to our political ability. I do not think that I exaggerate if I say that our history is one of the most interesting——we are fine fellows, but we often make a false step. I find the German anthropologists' skull and brain indices place us among the foremost nations——we are gifted, no doubt about that, but we are somewhat unstable, not circumspect enough, and shall I say, politically green; and political inexperience is a fertile soil for demagogy, and of that we have more than enough. The discussions about the crisis of democracy, and the shortcomings of parliamentary government have to a large extent their origin in that insufficient experience; and from that also that parrot-like imitation of foreign political isms——in short, we do not think enough according to our own selves, and to what is ours. In the Austrian times we got used to the negation of the state——that was the result of the subjugation; we even made ourselves believe that we could not any longer be independent. Well, no not that, with that idea I could never become reconciled; but I knew that subject people, depressed and deformed by subjugation do not

easily become free in spirit too at the wave of a
hand. That is why so many people among us
even today repudiate the state—by distrust, by
resistance to the state administration, by their
bad relations with whole strata of co-citizens—
to put it frankly: there are still some who side
with the thief rather than the policeman. Our
people have a patriotic tradition, it is true, but
on many occasions they are still too indifferent
to the state, against the state, almost anarchical;
they don't realize that it is the attitude of the old
Austrian spirit. To de-Austrianize, that means
to acquire a sense for the state, and what it
stands for, for the democratic state. That we
must ask not only from the bureaucracy, and
the army, but also from all citizens. And not
only the Czechs and the Slovaks.

Democracy must be livelier and sprightlier
than the old régime—especially that one of ours.
We must always bear in mind that we are a
small nation in an unfavourable geographical
position; in effect it imposes upon us the obliga-
tion to be more alert, to think more, to achieve
more than the others; or according to Palacky:
every self-respecting Czech and Slovak must do
three times as much as the members of big and
more favourably situated nations. Only bear in
mind that every educated fellow countryman of

ours needs to learn at least two foreign languages —how much time it takes, and work, but also what a gain it is not only for education but also for practical intercourse with nations! And so it is in everything: if we have to hold our own with honour we must thoroughly intensify all our political and cultural endeavour. Yes, it is a painstaking job; but who does not want to take trouble, don't let him talk of nation and patriotism.

Real love for one's nation is a very beautiful thing; with a decent and honest man it comes as a matter of course; therefore he does not talk much about it, just like a decent man does not go trumpeting abroad his love for his wife, family, and so on. A real love protects, bears sacrifices —and chiefly works. And for that work for the nation and state, a clear, sensible political, and cultural programme is necessary—mere daydreaming and getting excited is not enough. There is, after all, a difference between patriotism and jingoism; how much already did Havlíček struggle with that market-place jingoism, but for many it is as if he had never lived!

We must express our patriotism by a conscious public spirit. No doubt the state is ours, it is ours in virtue of historical right, according to the principle of the majority, and by the title that we have built it; but we have considerable minorities, and therefore we must be conscious of the difference between a state, and a nation: a nation is a cultural organization, a state a political organization. We have duties towards the nation, and we have duties towards the state. Obviously they must not conflict. We have built that state, we must know how to manage and govern it; it is our task to win over to the idea of our democratic republic the minorities with whom we are living. Their numbers, and their civilization, impose both on them and on us a democratic concord. Our procedure with the minorities is practically given to us by our own experience under Austria-Hungary: what we did not like to be done unto us, we shall not do unto others. The programme of Palacký, the father of the nation, is valid for us, and for those to come. Our history, the policy of the Premyslids, of St. Venceslas, Charles, and George must be a model for the policy with our Germans. The fact that we are surrounded on all sides by a big German neighbour, impels a thoughtful Czech to cautious and definitely wise politics.

Isn't there sometimes a conflict between the love for one's nation and for humanity, or rather: between nationalism and the humanitarian ideals like pacifism, mutual understanding between nations, and such-like things?

Between the love for one's nation, the love for one's country, and humanity there is no disagreement; as it is, it is between modern nationalism and humanity. Already that new and foreign word indicates that patriotism as our revivalists demanded it, and lived it, is something different from the nationalism of today.

As far as our national programme is concerned, remember what I told you with regard to the development of Europe, and to our own history, that is that we must take a hand in world politics, and consequently be in lively and friendly contact with other nations. Our national revival is a child of Enlightenment and of late Romanticism, it sprang from the humanitarian ideals of the Eighteenth and Nineteenth Centuries which were broadcast in France, in Germany, everywhere, Humanity—that is indeed our national programme, the programme of Dobrovský, Havlíček, and of Komenský in his day, of our kings George, and Charles, and of St. Venceslas.

Humanity does not exclude, or weaken the love for one's nation; I can, nay, I must love my nation positively, but because of that I need not hate other nations. True love is not proved by hatred, but only by love. Mankind is a sum of nations, it is not something outside the nations, and above them. Humanity, love, not only for one's neighbours, but for mankind—how am I to imagine that mankind concretely? I see a poor child that I can help—that child is mankind to me. The community with which I share its troubles, the nation with which I am combined through speech and culture is mankind. Mankind is simply a greater, or smaller sum of people for whom we can do something positive in deed, and not only in words. Humanity does not consist in day-dreaming about the whole of mankind, but in always acting humanely. If I ask politics to serve mankind, I do not infer that they ought not to be national, but just and decent. That's all.

Not as individuals, not as nations are we here merely to fulfil our egoistic aims. A nation that wished to live only for itself would be just as miserable as a man who wanted to live only for himself. Without faith in ideas and in ideals the life of men and of nations is only stagnation.

This, of course, is the political credo of an idealist.

Not at all, my boy: of a realist, in philosophy and in politics. For me politically realism meant: don't bury yourself in the recollection of a glorious past, work for a glorious present; don't put your faith only in words and slogans, for then you can improve the realities, and bring them to order; don't fly up in the clouds, but stick to your earth, it is the safest and least uncertain. Whatever you work for, stick to reality——

Only reality?

Yes; but without doubt reality also means spirituality, soul, love, moral order, God, and eternity. Only with them do we live an entire life, in full and complete reality, whether it be the life of an individual, or the history of nations. That full life alone is without inner conflict, such a life alone has a true and clear meaning——

and is a happy life.

Yes.

OVERLEAF

particulars of publications
of similar interest
issued by

GEORGE ALLEN & UNWIN LTD
LONDON: 40 MUSEUM STREET, W.C.1
LEIPZIG: (F. VOLCKMAR) HOSPITALSTR. 10
CAPE TOWN: 73 ST. GEORGE'S STREET
TORONTO: 91 WELLINGTON STREET, WEST
BOMBAY: 15 GRAHAM ROAD, BALLARD ESTATE
WELLINGTON, N.Z.: 8 KINGS CRESCENT, LOWER HUTT
SYDNEY, N.S.W.: AUSTRALIA HOUSE, WYNYARD SQUARE

Gladstone

by DR. ERICH EYCK

Demy 8vo   15s.

Sixty years of important political activity are vividly presented in Dr. Eyck's new life of Gladstone. The biography is dispassionate, up to date, and based on a critical study of sources of all the new material which has been made available since Morley's life. Gladstone is shown in his relations to the people important to his development: to the Queen, whose original warm appreciation turned to bitter aversion after the death of the Prince Consort, to Disraeli with whom he was engaged in constant political feud, to Palmerston, and to the tragic Parnell, with whose fate his own was interwoven. Throughout his career, Gladstone is shown as a man of resolute character, combining the arts of the practical statesman with the idealism of a great reformer and benefactor of mankind, and his progress is traced from a narrow Toryism to the full broad Liberalism of his later years.

"An authoritative but popular handbook of Gladstone."

"Gladstone stands out from Dr. Eyck's pages as, above all things, a man of principle and of honour."—*Reynolds News*

Rabindranath Tagore

PERSONALITY AND WORK

by PROFESSOR V. LESNY

La. Crown 8vo   8s. 6d.

Professor Lesny's authoritative study of the personality and work of Rabindranath Tagore is based on personal acquaintanceship with the poet and upon specialized literary knowledge. The book opens with a personal letter from Tagore containing the following statement.

"It is nothing short of miraculous how in a short time you have entered into the spirit of the Bengali language and my writings. I have never seen such strong critical ability in any other foreigner."

All prices are net

LONDON: GEORGE ALLEN & UNWIN LTD